Hello and welcome!
Ich bin der Wordmaster.
Hey!
Wir helfen dir beim Wörter lernen.
Nachdem neue Wörter in der Schule besprochen hast, kannst du die **New words** in diesem Buch als Vokabelheft benutzen.
Es gibt auch lustige Übungen. Die Lösungen findest du im beigelegten Heftchen.
Das große R bedeutet Revision: auf Deutsch Wiederholung. Hier übst du Vokabeln, die du bereits früher gelernt hast.
Tipps für die New words
1 Schau dir die Lücken im englischen Satz an. Welche neuen Wörter könnten passen?
2 Schau dir dann den deutschen Satz an. Die **fett gedruckten** Wörter zeigen, auf welches Wort es ankommt.
3 Wenn du mal nicht weiter weißt, kannst du auch im Vocabulary deines Schülerbuchs nachschlagen. Die Reihenfolge der Wörter dort hat dieselbe Reihenfolge wie die **New words**.
4 Im Vocabulary kannst du auch deine Lösungen überprüfen.
Introduction
New words ▸ p. 8
We use letters to ______ words.
Man ber
The Grand Canyon is a famous ______ .
Der Grand
I hate grey – ______ clothes are prettier.
Grau ma
The valley is about 20 ______ long.
The lake is more than 80 metres

Introduction

New words ▸ p. 8

We use letters to ___ words.	Man benutzt Buchstaben um Wörter zu **bilden**.
The Grand Canyon is a famous ___ .	Der Grand Canyon ist eine berühmte **Schlucht**.
I hate grey – ___ clothes are prettier.	Grau mag ich nicht – **bunte** Kleider sind schöner.
The valley is about 20 ___ long.	Das Tal ist ungefähr 20 **Kilometer** lang.
The lake is more than 80 metres ___ .	Der See ist über 80 Meter **tief**.
He looked at me over the ___ of his glasses.	Er schaute mich über den **Rand** seiner Brille an.
closed to the ___ on Mondays	montags für die **Öffentlichkeit** geschlossen
Everyone can use the ___ libraries.	Jeder darf die **öffentlichen** Bibliotheken benutzen.
go ___ on the Colorado River	auf dem Colorado **Floß fahren**
Rock climbing is the ___ adventure!	Felsklettern ist das **ultimative** Abenteuer!
___ are often stronger than horses.	**Maultiere** sind oft stärker als Pferde.
Does the price ___ breakfast?	**Schließt** der Preis das Frühstück **ein**?
Are you looking for hotel ___ ?	Suchen Sie nach einer Hotel**unterkunft**?

1 Word families

a) Finde die passenden Adjektive zu den angegebenen Nomen.

1 friend – friendly
2 colour – ___
3 difference – ___
4 horror – ___
5 cloud – ___
6 electricity – ___
7 danger – ___
8 day – ___
9 public – ___
10 crowd – ___

b) Vervollständige die Sätze mit einem Adjektiv oder einem Nomen aus der Liste in a).

1 Everybody gave me a very ___ welcome.
2 What's the ___ between a raft and a canoe?
3 The female bird is mainly brown, but the male is much more ___ .
4 Our local ___ library has a very good selection of books and DVDs.
5 People watched in ___ as the plane crashed.

New words ▸ p. 9

I always ____________ our holiday.	Ich **freue mich** immer **auf** unseren Urlaub.
The *Times* is a famous ________ newspaper.	Die *Times* is eine berühmte **Tages**zeitung.
stay for ____________ to three weeks	**zweieinhalb** bis drei Wochen bleiben
The show was ________ – everyone cheered.	Die Show war **klasse** – alle klatschten Beifall.
You can go riding or ______ in the mountains.	Man kann reiten oder in den Bergen **wandern**.
take part in a 15-kilometre ________	an einer 15-Kilometer **Wanderung** teilnehmen

2 Word search

Finde 20 englische Begriffe aus dem Wortfeld „Landschaft" und übersetze sie ins Deutsche. (↓ →)

valley – Tal

O	C	V	A	L	L	E	Y	G	W	J	I
B	O	I	C	S	F	O	R	E	S	T	S
E	C	L	W	A	T	E	R	F	A	L	L
A	A	L	A	K	E	C	L	I	F	F	A
C	N	A	S	C	E	N	E	R	Y	H	N
H	A	G	X	I	D	X	T	S	I	I	D
R	L	E	E	I	W	R	O	C	K	L	T
I	G	U	C	T	O	P	A	R	K	L	U
V	O	J	O	M	O	U	N	T	A	I	N
E	R	W	A	J	D	X	O	K	M	T	N
R	G	W	S	K	S	E	A	A	Q	X	E
L	E	Q	T	T	Z	D	V	P	K	I	L

New words ▸ p. 10

the __________ life of the Sioux around 1800	das **Stammes**leben der Sioux um 1800
German __________ fought against the Romans.	Deutsche **Stämme** kämpften gegen die Römer.
You need __________________ to borrow films.	Du brauchst einen **Ausweis** um Filme auszuleihen.
After the fire the house was a __________ .	Nach dem Brand war das Haus eine **Ruine**.
Today most Sioux live on __________________ .	Heute leben die meisten Sioux in **Reservaten.**
a 12-hour __________ from Bonn to Italy	eine 12-stündige **Autofahrt** von Bonn nach Italien
I'm __________ to hear you're well.	Ich bin **froh** zu hören, dass es dir gut geht.
I love hot soup, __________________ in winter.	Ich esse gern heiße Suppe, **besonders** im Winter.
Many ______________________ live in Alaska.	Viele **amerikanische Ureinwohner** leben in Alaska.

3 Spot the mistakes

In jedem Satz sind zwei Fehler. Unterstreiche und korrigiere sie.

1 About for million people visits the National Park each year. four ______________ ______________

2 The overnight mule traps include meals and accomodation. ______________ ______________

3 You can go on long heiks to diffrent places. ______________ ______________

4 What's the name from the river that runs threw the Canyon? ______________ ______________

5 Our visit to the reservat was really awsome. ______________ ______________

4 The best word

Finde in jeder Schublade das Wort, das am besten in die Lücke passt.

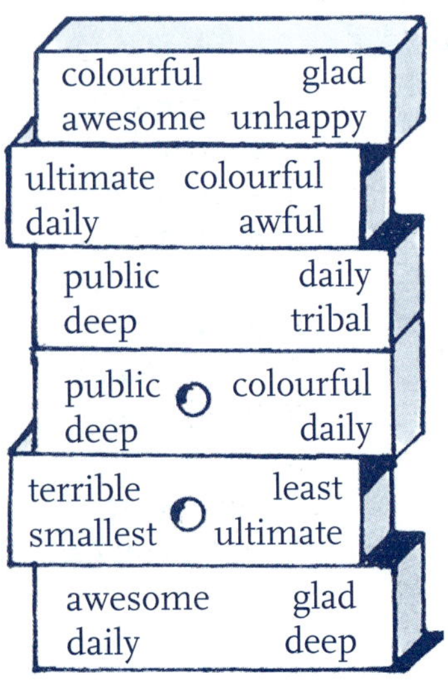

1 I'm so glad ______________ you were able to come.

2 Traditional Native American costumes are very ______________ .

3 It's a ______________ path – anyone can use it.

4 The dog fell into a ______________ hole and couldn't get out.

5 Rafting down the river will be the ______________ adventure.

6 We're interested in ______________ life on the reservation.

5 More about ... The Grand Canyon Skywalk

Vervollständige den Text mit den Wörtern aus der Liste.

allowed
build
includes
kind
popular
shape
special
sticks
public
take
through
tribe

The Skywalk is a ____________ (1) of bridge in the ____________ (2) of a *horseshoe. It is made of steel and glass and ____________ (3) out about 20 metres over the rim of one of the Grand Canyon's side canyons. Although it is strong enough to hold 800 people, only 120 are ____________ (4) on it at the same time. There's a great view into the Grand Canyon and you can also look ____________ (5) the glass floor to the ground over 1,000 metres below. But you aren't allowed to ____________ (6) photographs and you have to wear ____________ (7) shoes to *protect the floor.

The Skywalk belongs to the Hualapai, an Indian ____________ (8). It took three years to build it and, in March 2007, it opened to the ____________ (9). Tickets cost about $25, but you also have to pay over $50 for a one-mile bus trip, although this ____________ (10) lunch. The Skywalk is perhaps expensive, but it is ____________ (11) with tourists. The Hualapai plan to ____________ (12) a museum, shops and hotels at the same place.

horseshoe = Hufeisen; protect= schützen

6 Last letter – first letter

Der letzte Buchstabe von jedem Wort ist gleichzeitig der erste des nächsten Wortes.

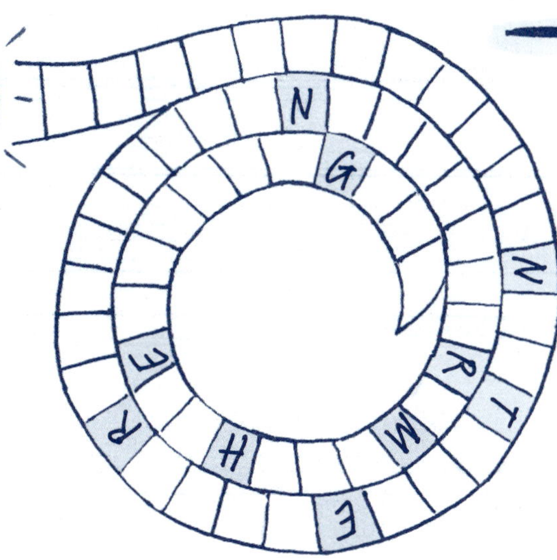

1 Unterkunft
2 gepflegt
3 Volksstamm
4 Redakteur
5 Reservat
6 Nachbar
7 Kante, Rand
8 Wettkampf
9 wandern
10 aufregend
11 froh, dankbar

New words ▸ p. 11

Students in ___________ 8 are about 14 years old.	Schüler in **Klasse** 8 sind ungefähr 14 Jahre alt.
___________________ money for a charity	Geld für eine Wohlfahrtsorganisation **sammeln**
Dad ___________________ in the garden every week.	Im Garten **mäht** Papa jede Woche den **Rasen.**
Sheep and cows eat lots of ______________ .	Schafe und Kühe fressen viel **Gras.**
You can buy lots of things cheaply at a ________ .	Im **Schlussverkauf** kann man vieles billig kaufen.
There was no hotel, so we slept in ______________ .	Es gab kein Hotel, daher schliefen wir in **Zelten.**
Juice or lemonade? – I _____________ juice.	Saft oder Limonade? – Ich **bevorzuge** Saft.
Do you know ______________ open this door?	Weißt du, **wie man** diese Tür öffnet?
use ____________________________ to watch birds	**ein Fernglas** benutzen um Vögel zu beobachten
He needs ______________ to repair the clock.	Er braucht **Werkzeuge**, um die Uhr zu reparieren.
She did it ___________________ – without any help.	Sie hat es **allein** gemacht – ohne jede Hilfe.
Can you ___________ a button on for me, please?	Kannst du mir bitte einen **Knopf** annähen?

7 Words in pictures: outdoor activities

Wie heißen die Gegenstände? Bei welcher Aktivität kann man sie benutzen?

1 boots – hiking

2 ______________________

3 ______________________

4 ______________________

5 ______________________

6 ______________________

7 ______________________

8 ______________________

9 ______________________

10 ______________________

New words ▸ p. 12

the fastest __________ from Cologne to Berlin	die schnellste **Strecke** von Köln nach Berlin
No car moves without __________ .	Ohne **Benzin** fährt kein Auto.
You get oil and air at __________ .	An **Tankstellen** bekommt man Öl und Luft.
__________ are a kind of ID for cars.	**Nummernschilder** sind eine Art Ausweis für Autos.
We're just crossing the __________ to Texas.	Gerade überqueren wir die **Grenze** nach Texas.
Do you keep __________ on this farm?	Halten Sie **Vieh** auf dieser Farm?
__________ lived million years ago.	**Dinosaurier** lebten vor Millionen Jahren.
a huge __________ of model planes	eine riesige **Sammlung** von Modellflugzeugen
After a long drive we __________ arrived.	Nach einer langen Fahrt kamen wir **endlich** an.
There's a __________ view from here.	Von hier hat man einen **eindrucksvollen** Ausblick.
We were tired and went __________ to bed.	Wir waren müde und gingen **direkt** ins Bett.
The hills __________ as far as we could see.	Die Hügel **erstreckten sich** so weit wir sehen konnten.
five or six __________ of __________-coloured rock	fünf oder sechs **Schichten** von **mehr**farbigen Felsen
We walked along the mountain __________ .	Wir spazierten den Berg**pfad** entlang.
He's six __________ tall – that's about 1 metre 83.	Er ist sechs **Fuß** groß – das sind etwa 1 Meter 83.
a beach at the northern __________ of the island	ein Strand an der nördlichen **Spitze** der Insel
Birds have two __________ .	Vögel haben zwei **Flügel**.
Please __________ me. I didn't want to hurt you.	Bitte **vergib** mir! Ich wollte dich nicht verletzen.
a short __________ at London airport	ein kurzer **Aufenthalt** am Londoner Flughafen
on the busy __________ to New York	auf der verkehrsreichen **Fernstraße** nach New York

8 Odd word out

Ein Wort passt nicht. Finde und unterstreiche es.

1 road – border – route – highway

2 toes – feet – centimetres – miles

3 accommodation – finally – first – later

4 deep – glad – long – high

5 tribe – valley – gorge – mountain

6 tent – caravan – villa – mule

7 canoe – cycle – include – hike

8 awful – awesome – fantastic – grand

9 horse – dinosaur – mule – zebra

10 slowly – quietly – carefully – especially

9 Scrambled words: American and British English

Die Buchstabenrätsel ergeben Wörter aus dem amerikanischen Englisch. Trage diese und ihre britischen Entsprechungen ein. Die Tipps helfen dir.

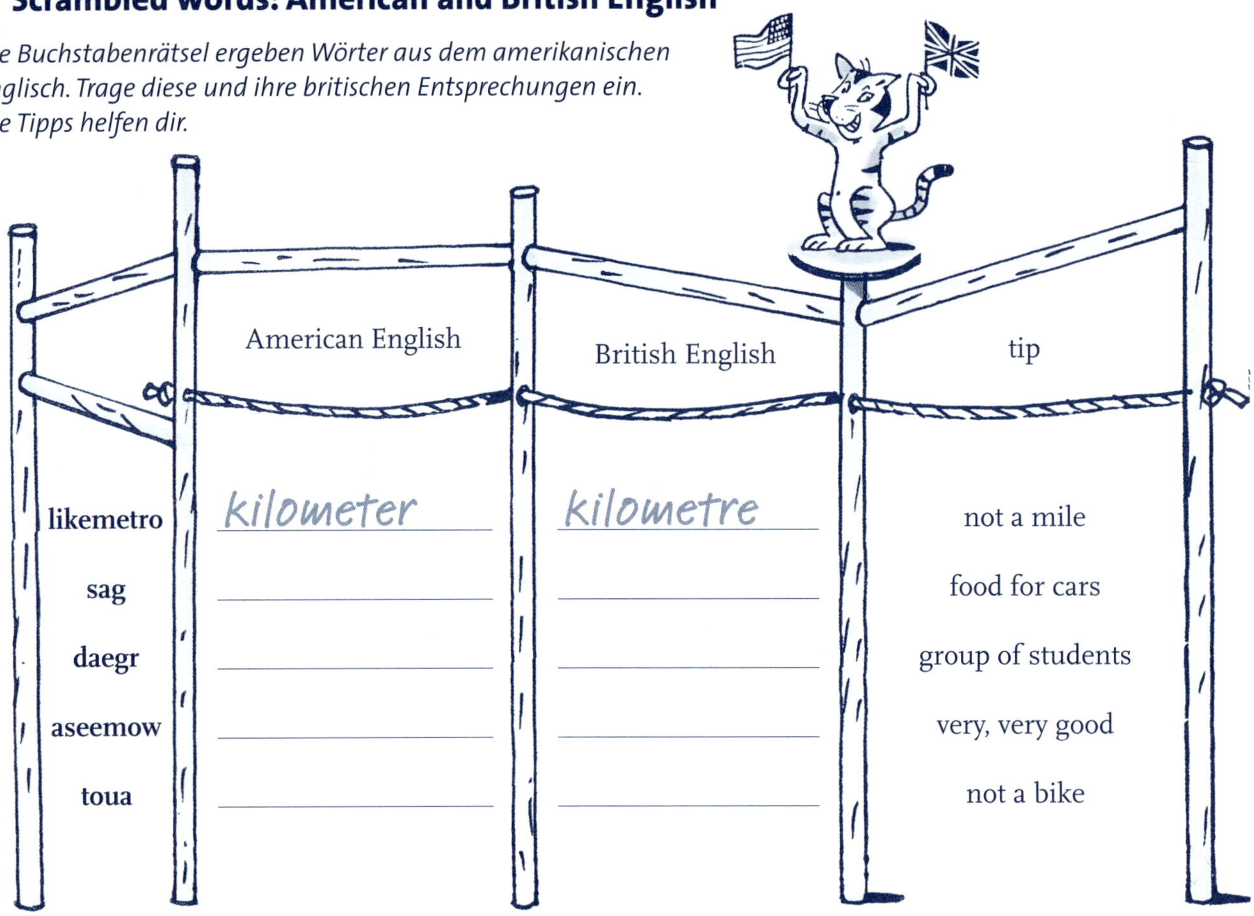

		American English	British English	tip
1	likemetro	kilometer	kilometre	not a mile
2	sag			food for cars
3	daegr			group of students
4	aseemow			very, very good
5	toua			not a bike

10 Crossword

Trage die Übersetzungen der deutschen Wörter ins Rätsel ein.

Across
1 froh, dankbar (4)
4 Ruine (4)
5 Fels, Felsen (4)
7 Grenze (6)
9 direkt (8)
11 Zelt (4)
13 täglich (5)
14 vorziehen (6)

Down
1 Schlucht (5)
2 wandern (4)
3 öffentlich (6)
6 Vieh (6)
8 Rand (3)
10 Stamm (4)
11 Werkzeug (4)
12 Spitze (3)
13 tief (4)

New words ▸ p. 15

____________ into the US from Mexico	die **Einwanderung** in die USA aus Mexico
Many ____________ hope for a new life.	Viele **Einwanderer** hoffen auf ein neues Leben.
He ____________ into the US to find work.	Er **wanderte** in die USA **ein**, um Arbeit zu finden.
a wide ____________ with shops and cafés	eine breite **Allee** mit Läden und Cafés
We have the ____________ to say what we think.	Wir haben die **Freiheit** zu sagen, was wir denken.

1 Number crossword

Gleiche Zahlen sind gleiche Buchstaben. Die angegebenen Lösungen helfen dir, das gesamte Rätsel zu lösen.

Wo im Rätsel findet man das englische Wort für ...

öffentlich j across

Vieh k down

Maultier ____________

Grenze ____________

Zelt ____________

Benzin ____________

Rand, Kante ____________

Flügel ____________

Werkzeug ____________

wetten ____________

einschließen ____________

anhalten ____________

Badewanne ____________

Spitze ____________

New words ▸ p. 16

walk around the ________ with the dog	mit dem Hund um den **Block** laufen
I'm cold and I'm ________ hungry.	Ich friere und bin **auch** hungrig.
travel on the ________________	mit dem **Bus in Richtung Stadtzentrum** fahren
the ________ from here to the moon	die **Entfernung** von hier zum Mond
cross the road at the ________________	die Straße am **Fußgängerüberweg** überqueren
Two ________ were killed by a car.	Zwei **Fußgänger** wurden von einem Auto getötet.
I stood in a long ________ outside the cinema.	Ich stand in einer langen **Schlange** vor dem Kino.
The ________ welcomed all her guests.	Die **Gastgeberin** begrüßte alle ihre Gäste.
A good ________ looks after his guests.	Ein guter **Gastgeber** kümmert sich um seine Gäste.
Please don't ________ the park.	Bitte **lassen** Sie keine **Abfälle** im Park **zurück.**
Please throw your ________ in the bin.	Bitte wirf deinen **Abfall** in die Mülltonne.
Can I pay in US ________ ?	Kann ich in US-**Dollar** bezahlen?
The thief had to pay a high ________ .	Der Dieb musste eine hohe **Geldstrafe** bezahlen.

2 Hidden words

Ergänze die Wortgruppen, indem du Wörter mit Buchstaben aus dem Begriff „pedestrian" bildest.

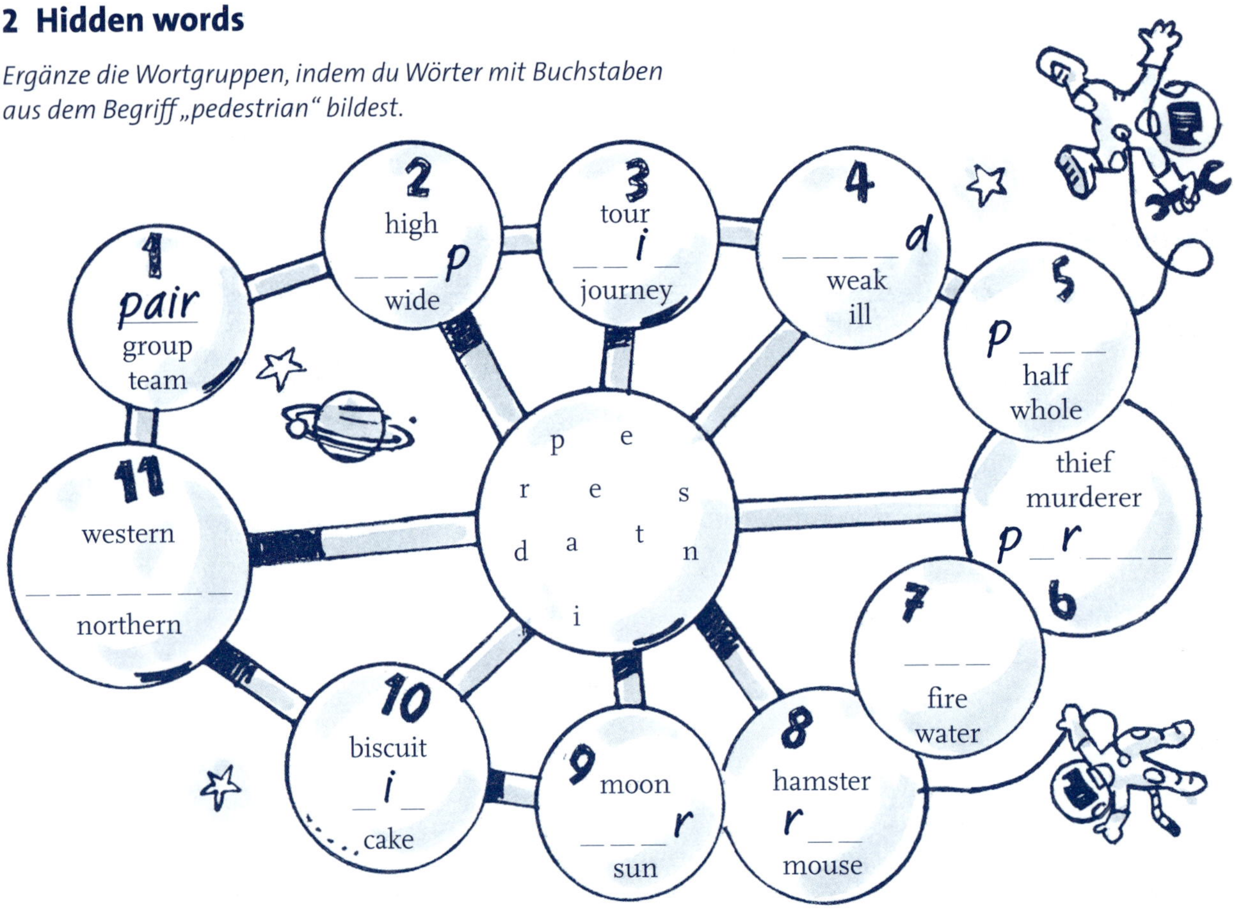

3 Definitions

Vervollständige die Definitionen mit Wörtern aus der linken Sprühwolke. Trage die Lösungen aus der anderen Sprühwolke in die rechte Spalte ein.

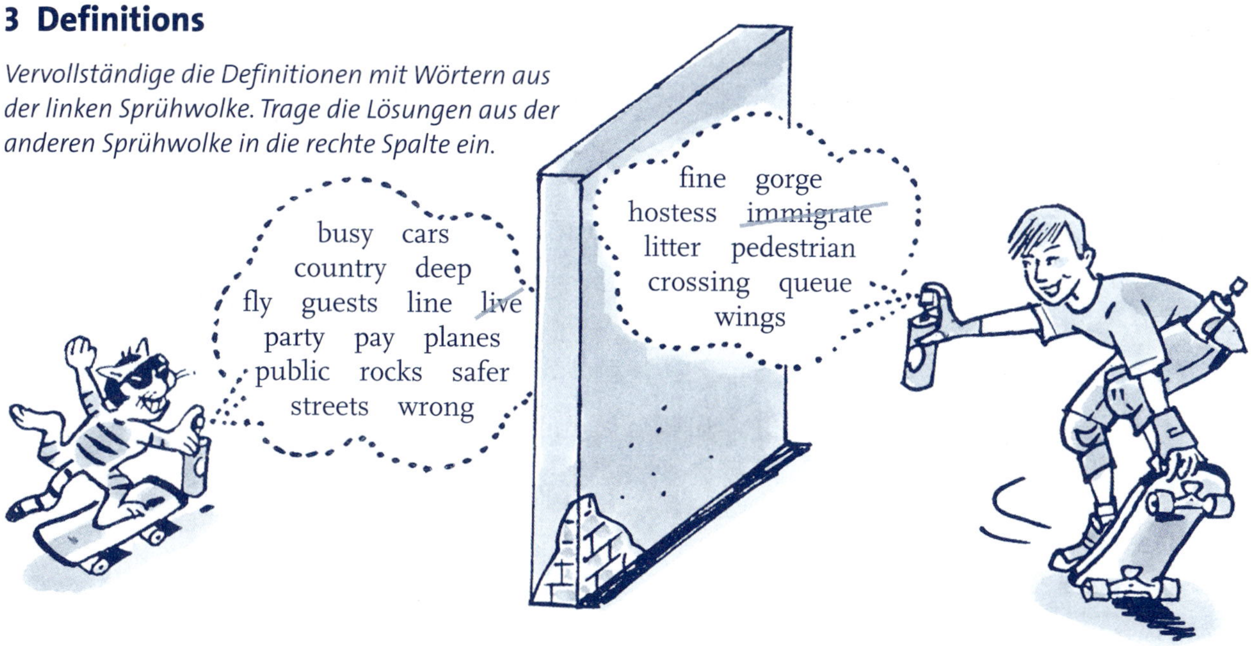

1	come and live in a ______ after leaving your own country	immigrate
2	a place where it's ______ to cross a ______ street	______
3	a ______ of people or ______ waiting for something	______
4	a woman who invites ______ to a ______ at her house	______
5	money you must ______ if you do something ______	______
6	rubbish which is left on ______ or other ______ places	______
7	something that birds and ______ need to ______	______
8	a ______ valley with ______ and usually a river	______

4 Opposites

Trage die Gegenteile der fettgedruckten Wörter in die zweite Spalte ein. Ergänze die Tabelle mit den englischen Oberbegriffen und deren deutschen Übersetzungen.

1 **near**	far		Entfernung
2 **happy**		feeling	
3 **loud**			Klang
4 **late**			
5 **warm**			
6 **large**			
7 **black**			
8 **young**			

New words ▸ p. 17

70 firemen work at the ____________________ .	70 Feuerwehrmänner arbeiten auf der **Feuerwache.**
Put on a coat – ______________ you'll be cold.	Zieh einen Mantel an – **sonst** wirst du frieren.
Over 20 _________________ hurried to the fire.	Über 20 **Feuerwehrleute** eilten zum Brand.
You need water to _________________ a fire.	Man braucht Wasser, um ein Feuer zu **löschen.**
work on the night ____________ at a factory	Nacht**schicht** in einer Fabrik arbeiten
____________ was a terrible day for the US.	**Nine Eleven** war ein schrecklicher Tag für die USA.
The ____________ have just killed a passenger.	Die **Entführer** haben gerade einen Passagier getötet.
At 25 he _______________ his father's company.	Mit 25 **übernahm** er die Firma seines Vaters.
The new ________________ will be 612 m high.	Der neue **Wolkenkratzer** wird 612 m hoch sein.
Fires were _______________ all over the forest.	Im ganzen Wald **brannten** Feuer.
The old man _________________ and died.	Der alte Mann **brach zusammen** und starb.

5 Word search – In a city

Finde 15 Begriffe aus dem Wortfeld „Stadt". (↓ →)
Übersetze sie ins Deutsche.
Kennzeichne 4 Begriffe aus dem amerikanischen Englisch mit AE.

S	S	D	O	W	N	T	O	W	N	H	W
T	I	S	K	Y	S	C	R	A	P	E	R
A	D	H	M	Z	M	U	S	E	U	M	C
T	E	O	B	Y	S	Y	Q	Z	M	J	R
U	W	S	K	G	R	Y	U	Y	M	Q	O
E	A	P	F	A	Y	C	A	R	L	B	S
R	L	I	O	U	K	Z	R	Q	I	R	S
D	K	T	S	N	U	C	E	M	B	I	W
W	F	A	P	V	F	J	M	V	R	D	A
C	O	L	A	V	E	N	U	E	A	G	L
H	U	A	R	B	L	O	C	K	R	E	K
B	A	N	K	S	U	B	W	A	Y	H	E

statue – Statue

6 Pronunciation

Wie wird das /a/ ausgesprochen? Ordne die Wörter aus der Box der richtigen Aussprachegruppe zu.

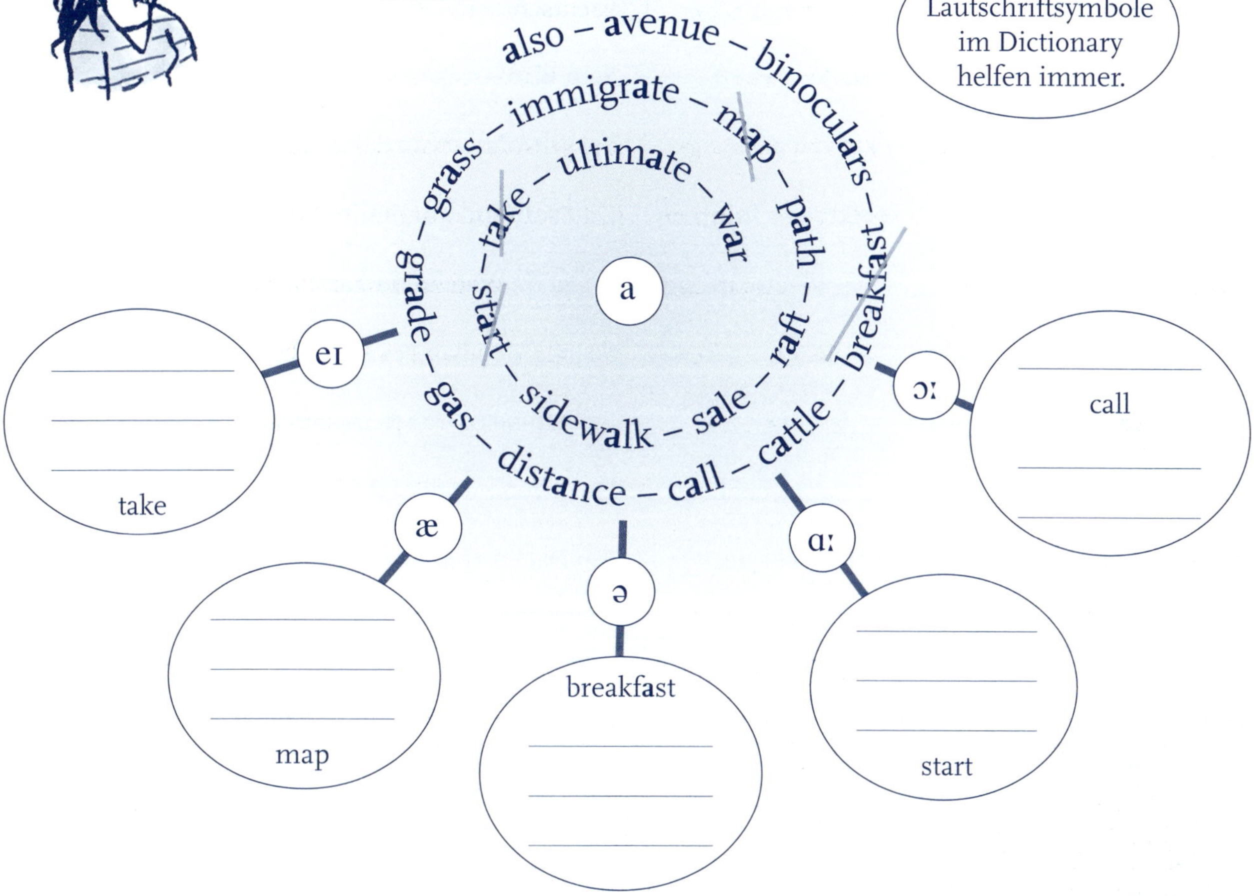

7 The fourth word

Welches Wort fehlt hier?

1 house – hall	hotel – lobby	*9* 14–18 – high school	11–14 – ________
2 walk – feet	fly – ________	*10* wind – blow	fire – ________
3 finger – hand	toe – ________	*11* food – supermarket	petrol – ________
4 Germany – euro	US – ________	*12* run – runner	immigrate – ________
5 Germany – kilometre	US – ________	*13* chicken – meat	salmon – ________
6 small – large	short – ________	*14* lunch – meal	chili con carne – ________
7 GB – ground floor	US – ________	*15* firefighters – fire station	police – ________
8 top – above	bottom – ________	*16* sing – song	sell – ________

New words ▸ p. 18

New York is the ________ city ___ the country.	New York ist die **größte** Stadt **des** Landes.
Hot and sunny! ________ weather for the beach.	Heiß und sonnig! **Ideales** Wetter für den Strand.
meet in the hotel ____________	sich in der **Eingangshalle** des Hotels treffen
So much fog! ____________ is very poor.	So viel Nebel! Die **Sichtweite** ist sehr schlecht.
buy tickets at the ________________	Fahrkarten an der **Kasse** kaufen
His office is right at the top – four __________ .	Sein Büro ist ganz oben – vier **Stockwerke höher**.
They were ____________ with fear.	Sie **schwitzten** vor Furcht.
______________ ! Nobody was injured!	**Gott sei Dank**! Keiner wurde verletzt!
Do you want to wait __________ till Sue comes?	Willst du **eine Weile** warten, bis Sue kommt?
Be quiet! I'm ____________ listening to you.	Sei still! Ich **habe es satt**, dir zuzuhören.
Shall I help? No, I can do it ____________ .	Soll ich helfen? – Nein, ich kann es **selbst** machen.
Hollywood is the world's __________ capital.	Hollywood ist die **Film**hauptstadt der Welt.
A __________ is a kind of tropical forest.	Ein **Dschungel** ist eine Art tropischer Wald.
Can the lion ____________ from the cage?	Kann der Löwe aus dem Käfig **entkommen**?
Many people believe in life after __________ .	Viele Leute glauben an ein Leben nach dem **Tod**.
He cycles every day, __________ the weather.	Er fährt jeden Tag Fahrrad, **egal welches** Wetter.
This skyscraper is the ________ in the world.	Dieser Wolkenkratzer ist der **höchste** der Welt.
Knock before you __________ the room.	Klopf an, bevor du den Raum **betrittst**.
The ________________ is on the top floor.	Die **Aussichtsplattform** ist im obersten Stockwerk.
He __________ me money, but I didn't take it.	Er hat mir Geld **angeboten**, aber ich nahm es nicht.
You get a ____________ view from the top.	Von oben hat man eine **spektakuläre** Aussicht.
You often feel ____________ on car doors.	Oft spürt man **elektrische Aufladung** an Autotüren.
We built a __________ around our garden.	Wir bauten einen **Zaun** um unseren Garten.
She ________ her mother and said good night.	Sie **küsste** ihre Mutter und sagte gute Nacht.
There was only a small __________ of hope.	Es gab nur einen kleinen **Funken** Hoffnung.
white teeth and red __________	weiße Zähne und rote **Lippen**

8 Lost words

Ergänze die Sätze mit den Wörtern auf dem Skateboard.

1 There's a library near you wherever you live in New York.

2 I didn't cook the whole meal ___________ – my sister helped me.

3 I live just outside London, not in London ___________ .

4 Jake runs in the park every morning ___________ the weather.

5 That's a very nice blouse. Did you really make it ___________ ?

6 ___________ is making all that noise – please stop!

7 I'm sure you'll find your rucksack ___________ you left it.

8 I didn't see the queen ___________ , but I saw one of the princes.

9 Just phone me ___________ your plane arrives.

10 The school disco is organised by the students ___________

9 Word ladder

Gehe von unten nach oben, indem du auf jeder Sprosse einen Buchstaben veränderst.

These jeans were really cheap in the winter ★.

Is that dog a ★ or a female?

I want to ride a ★ at the Grand Canyon.

1 ★ = 1609 metres

This pen isn't ★ – is it yours?

★ your own business!

Cycling against the ★ was difficult.

That poor bird can't fly – it's hurt its left ★.

The ★ and queen have just arrived.

It was ★ of scary alone in the park at night.

Did you ★ the book you were looking for?

Dad had to pay a ★ for driving too fast.

BE queue = AE ★

What kind of music do you ★?

We went on a long ★ in the mountains.

New words ▸ p. 19

Lots of New Yorkers eat ___ as a snack.	Viele New Yorker essen **Bagels** als Imbiss.
Bagels and ___ are very popular.	Bagels mit **Frischkäse** sind sehr beliebt.
Do you prefer milk or ___ ?	Nimmst du lieber Milch oder **Sahne**?
There's no fruit yogurt – just ___ yogurt.	Es gibt keinen Fruchtjoghurt – nur **Naturjoghurt**.
Would you prefer tea or ___ ?	Möchtest du lieber Tee oder **Kaffee**?
A shop assistant stood behind the ___ .	Eine Verkäuferin stand hinter der **Theke**.
The sauce smells good and ___ even better.	Die Soße riecht gut und **schmeckt** noch besser.
I never drink tea because I hate the ___ .	Ich trinke nie Tee, weil ich den **Geschmack** hasse.
Don't hurry. We've got ___ time!	Beeilt euch nicht. Wir haben **reichlich** Zeit!
Judy ___ me a shy ___ .	Judy **lächelte** mich schüchtern an.
Hanukkah is a ___ festival.	Chanukka ist ein **jüdisches** Fest.
put tomatoes and cheese on the pizza ___	Tomaten und Käse auf den Pizza**teig** legen
Water ___ at 100 degrees.	Wasser **kocht** bei 100 Grad.
Put the cake in the hot ___ .	Den Kuchen in den heißen **Ofen** stellen.
Do you like cakes with a cream ___ ?	Magst du Kuchen mit Sahne**füllung**?
We ___ slowly around the park.	Wir **schlenderten** langsam im Park umher.

10 Word building

Verbinde ein Wort aus der Liste mit einem Wort von der Box. Trage die deutsche Übersetzung ein.

performer office spoon station man
plate ~~glasses~~ station session ~~cheese~~

1	cream cheese	Frischkäse	6	petrol ___	___
2	tea ___	___	7	sunglasses	___
3	ticket ___	___	8	street ___	___
4	training ___	___	9	fire ___	___
5	number ___	___	10	fire ___	___

New words ▸ *pp. 24–27*

A ________ writes articles in newspapers.	Ein **Journalist** schreibt Artikel in Zeitungen.
At 11 I ________ short ________ from work.	Um 11 **mache** ich **eine** kurze **Pause** von der Arbeit
________ vocabulary before the test	Vokabeln vor dem Test **wiederholen**
improve the first ________ of a text	den Erst**entwurf** eines Textes verbesseren
Where can small children play in ________ ?	Wo können kleine Kinder in **Sicherheit** spielen?
Try to ________ what the number means.	Versuche **herauszufinden**, was die Zahl bedeutet.
find a ________ for a text	eine **Überschrift** für einen Text finden
add a ________ to a word	eine **Nachsilbe** an ein Wort anfügen
show a word in its ________	ein Wort in seinem **Zusammenhang** zeigen
a special ________ for learning vocabulary	eine besondere **Technik**, um Wortschatz zu lernen

11 Scrambled words: American and British English

Die Buchstabenrätsel ergeben Wörter aus dem amerikanischen Englisch. Trage diese und ihre britischen Entsprechungen ein. Die Tipps helfen dir.

		American English	British English	tip
1	edgar	grade	class	group of students
2	busyaw			a kind of transport
3	askwilde			a path along the side of a road
4	elin			You often see them at bus stops.
5	odontwnw			a city's heart
6	patentram			home for lots of people
7	okcrasslw			You cross the street on it.
8	hiergnob			someone who lives near you

New words ▸ *p. 28*

The ________ landed the plane safely.	Der **Pilot** landete das Flugzeug sicher.
help the victims of ________	den Opfern des **Terrorismus** helfen
Open this door only in an ________ .	Öffnen Sie diese Tür nur im **Notfall**.
The ________ workers came by helicopter.	Der **Rettungsdienst** kam mit dem Hubschrauber.
The Sunday ________ starts at ten o'clock.	Der Sonntags**gottesdienst** beginnt um 10 Uhr.
________ a ________ in front of 500 people	eine **Rede** vor 500 Menschen **halten**
He's lonely. He ________ stay with him.	Er ist einsam. Er **möchte, dass ich** bei ihm bleibe.
She's so sad. How can we ________ her?	Sie ist so traurig! Wie können wir sie **trösten**?
John F. Kennedy was a famous ________ .	John F. Kennedy war ein berühmter **Politiker.**
I said hello but he didn't ________ me.	Ich grüßte ihn, aber er **erkannte** mich nicht.

12 Words with different meanings

Finde in der Liste die passenden Wörter zu den Paaren 1–8. Trage sie ein und unterstreiche die deutschen Entsprechungen.

break
~~flat~~
fine
floor
service
stop
tall
tip

1
a) in eine kleinere Wohnung ziehen
b) Man dachte früher, die Erde sei flach.
flat

2
a) eine Geldstrafe für zu schnelles Fahren
b) Ich fühle mich heute gut.
____

3
a) Der Service in diesem Laden ist sehr gut.
b) Das war ein schöner Gottesdienst.
____

4
a) Sollen wir hier einen Aufenthalt machen?
b) Hör auf, bitte!
____

5
a) die nördliche Spitze der Insel
b) ein guter Tipp für den Urlaub in New York
____

6
a) Das ist ein sehr hohes Gebäude.
b) Mein Bruder ist fast 2 Meter groß.
____

7
a) Kleider vom Boden aufheben
b) im 6. Stockwerk wohnen
____

8
a) eine kurze Pause machen
b) Gläser kaputt machen
____

13 More about ... Remembering 9/11

Vervollständige den Text mit den oben stehenden Wörtern.

although close help skyline who touch work on you whole

Every year on September 11, New York's ______________ (1) looks a little different. Between all the skyscrapers of Manhattan, ______________ (2) can see two huge columns of blue light – and these 'skyscrapers' really seem to reach the sky! On a cloudy day, they ______________ (3) the clouds and make them blue. The light comes from 88 very strong lamps ______________ (4) to where the World Trade Centre stood before terrorists destroyed it on September 11, 2001. This ______________ (5) of art is called 'Tribute in Light'. It was turned ______________ (6) for the first time in March 2002, when it lit up the sky for a ______________ (7) month. Now it is turned on just once a year, on September 11. Many New Yorkers like the two columns of light. They ______________ (8) them to remember the World Trade Centre's two huge towers and the people ______________ (9) died in the terrorist attacks. The 'Tribute in Light' costs $350,000 a year. ______________ (10) many people want to keep the tribute, at the moment it is not clear where the money will come from.

14 Hour glasses

Übersetze die Wörter und trage sie in die passende Sanduhr ein.

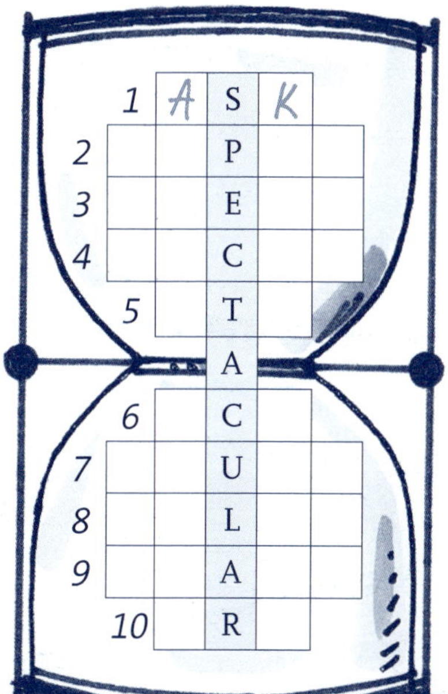

1 Nebel – fragen
2 Thema – Hütte
3 Sahne –schmecken
4 örtlich – schwitzen
5 versuchen – aß
6 verrückt – Eis
7 Teig – betreten
8 Wohnblock – Pilot
9 heiraten – Entwurf
10 schreien – Tschüss

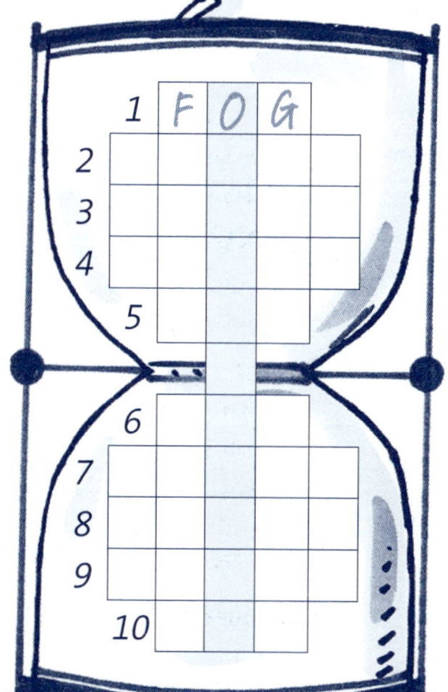

Das geheime Wort heißt: Englisch ______________________

Deutsch ______________________

New words ► p. 29

Did you ______ how she looked at you?	Hast du **bemerkt**, wie sie dich angeschaut hat?
Louis XIV was an ______ king.	Ludwig XIV. war ein **außergewöhnlicher** König.
In a difficult ______ you need help.	In einer schwierigen **Situation** braucht man Hilfe.
She's got ______ hair and green eyes.	Sie hat **rötliches** Haar und grüne Augen.
A head teacher is ______ other teachers.	Ein Schulleiter ist **ranghöher als** andere Lehrer.
The young pilot is ______ the captain.	Der junge Pilot ist dem Kapitän **untergeordnet**.
He's a person I can ______ on.	Er ist jemand, auf den ich mich **verlassen** kann.
I'm ______ – I do what I promise.	Ich bin **zuverlässig** – ich tue, was ich verspreche.
not really cold, but maybe ______ cool	nicht wirklich kalt, aber vielleicht **ein wenig** kühl
She's very ______ and often goes to church.	Sie ist sehr **gläubig** und geht oft in die Kirche.
learn something about the Jewish ______	etwas über die jüdische **Religion** erfahren
go to ______ every Sunday	jeden Sonntag zur **Messe** gehen
Is life ______ easier than 50 years ago?	Ist das Leben **heutzutage** leichter als vor 50 Jahren?
After the accident his life ______ .	Nach dem Unfall **veränderte** sich sein Leben.
My parents often ______ to drive.	Meine Eltern **wechseln** sich oft beim Fahren **ab**.
I've ______ some really great ideas.	Ich habe **mir** ein paar tolle Ideen **ausgedacht**.
He's a famous film and theatre ______ .	Er ist ein berühmter Film- und Theater**kritiker**.
Don't be so ______ to your sister.	Sei nicht so **gemein** zu deiner Schwester.
This church is named after ______ Mary.	Diese Kirche ist nach der **Heiligen** Maria benannt.

15 Verb forms

Ergänze die Tabelle der unregelmäßigen Verben.

1	take	took	taken
2		sewed	
3		left	
4	ring		
5		came	

6	forgive		
7		blew	
8			cut
9			felt
10		woke	

New words ▸ *p. 30*

He climbed the ______________ to the window.	Er kletterte die **Leiter** bis zum Fenster hinauf.
a ____________ hero without fear of death	ein **ehrenhafter** Held ohne Angst vor dem Tod
Stop ______________ – I know you're fantastic!	Hör auf **anzugeben** – ich weiß, dass du toll bist!
If you want ____________ , you have to pay for it.	Wenn du **Qualität** willst, muss du dafür bezahlen.
It's ______________ amazine, how well he sings.	Es ist **absolut** erstaunlich, wie gut er singt.
Tidy your books and _____ them ____________ .	Räume deine Bücher auf und **ordne** sie.
Has he got the __________ to play in goal?	Hat er die **Fähigkeit**, im Tor zu stehen?
I don't know how I can _______ the question.	Ich weiß nicht, wie ich die Frage **formulieren** soll.
important skills for this ___________________	wichtige Fähigkeiten für diese **berufliche Richtung**
Most people ___________________ a hero.	Die meisten Menschen **respektieren** einen Helden.
What you need is _________________ help.	Was du brauchst, ist **professionelle** Hilfe.
I stayed at home _________________ the rain.	**Wegen** des Regens blieb ich zu Hause.
It's a ______________ that nobody was hurt.	Es ist ein **Segen**, dass niemand verletzt wurde.
I _______ many friends _______ when I moved.	Als ich umzog, **ließ** ich viele Freunde **zurück**.

16 Word friends

In jedem Haus gibt es drei Wörter bzw. Wortverbindungen, die man direkt nach dem Verb auf der Fahne benutzen kann. Unterstreiche sie.

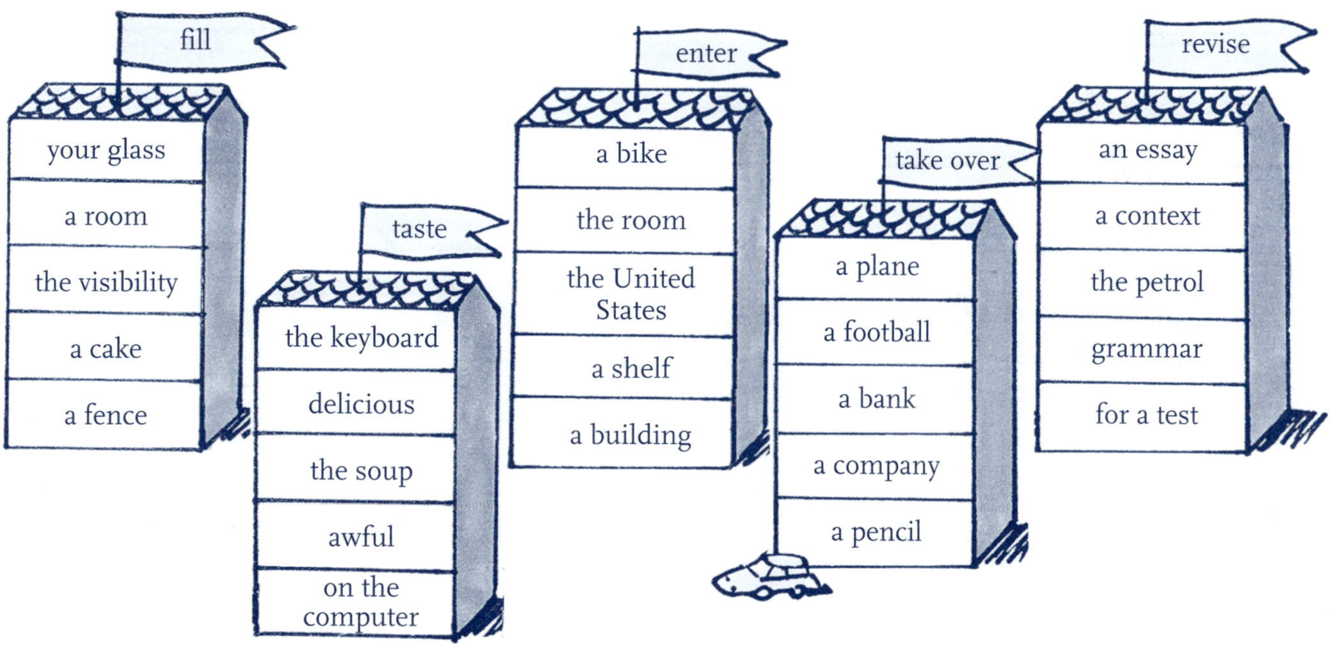

17 What are the words?

*Wie übersetzt man das Wort **change** ins Deutsche?*

1 Grandma never **changes**. She's as beautiful as ever. ______

2 We still have to **change** our pounds into dollars. ______

3 This film's boring. Can you **change** the station, please? ______

4 You don't have to **change** – that dress is fine. ______

5 We have to **change** at Waterloo Station. ______

6 I'd like to **change** to a room with a view of the sea. ______

18 Word groups

Trage die Wörter aus der Wolke in die richtigen Sterne ein.

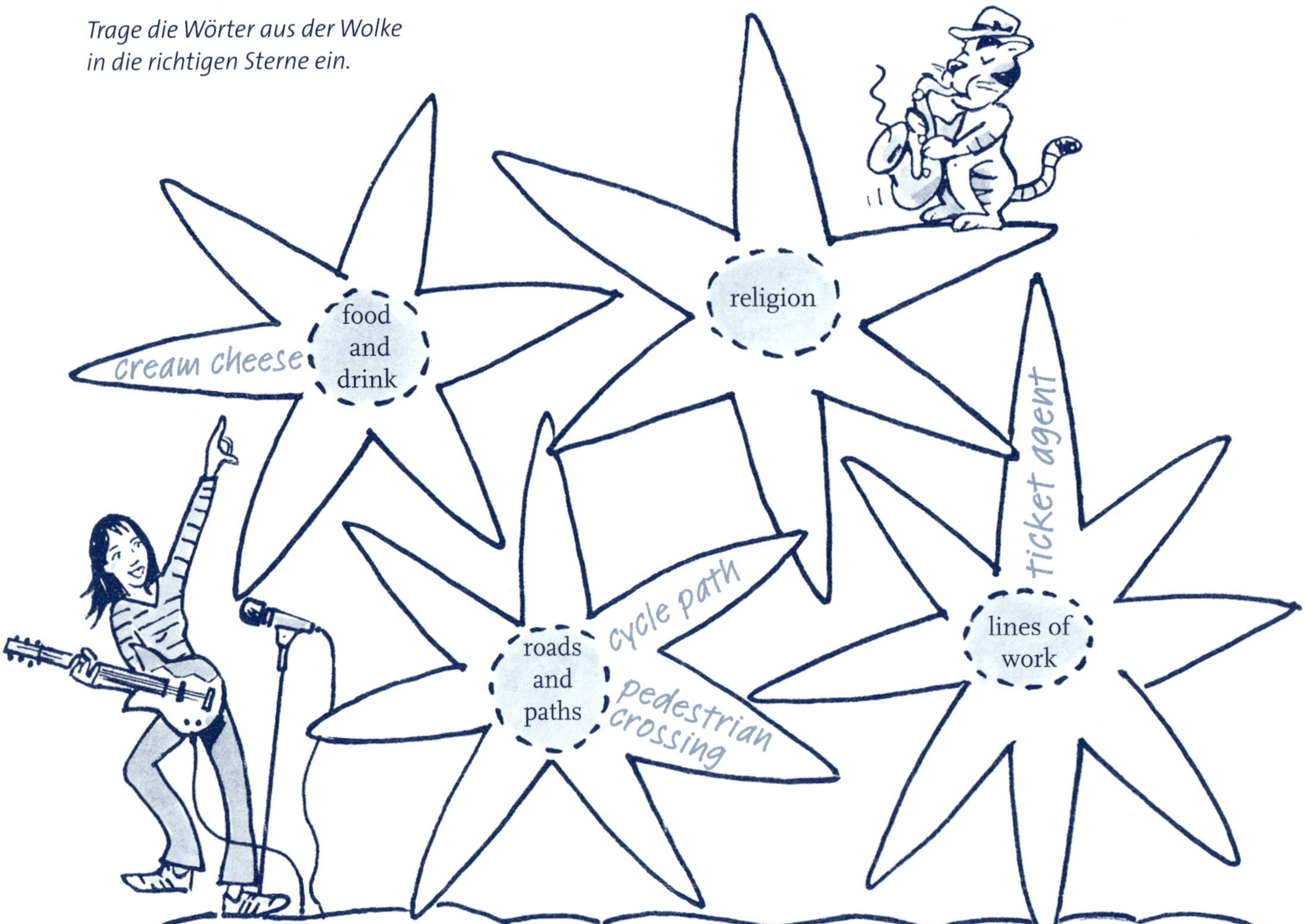

avenue – bagel – beef – blessing – cathedral – church – coffee – cream cheese – cycle path
dough – firefighter – hairdresser – highway – hostess – journalist – mass – mosque – musician
onion – pavement – pedestrian crossing – pilot – politician – roll – saint – salmon
service – street – synagogue – ticket agent – trail

New words ▸ pp. 36–37

Robin Hood hunted with ____________________ .	Robin Hood jagte mit **Pfeil und Bogen.**
The British often eat _____________ at Christmas.	Die Briten essen oft **Truthahn** an Weihnachten.
Lots of _____________ came from the fire.	Eine Menge **Rauch** kam aus dem Feuer.
Is there a clean __________________ for the table?	Gibt's eine saubere **Tischdecke** für den Tisch?
The Old Testament is a part of the _____________ .	Das alte Testament ist ein Teil der **Bibel.**
The __________ of the river is in the mountains.	Die **Quelle** des Flusses ist in den Bergen.
There are 15 _____________ on the birthday cake.	Es gibt 15 **Kerzen** auf dem Geburtstagskuchen.
Can you make cheese with __________'s milk?	Kann man aus **Ziegen**milch Käse machen?
Young girls often play with _____________ .	Junge Mädchen spielen oft mit **Puppen.**
Native American or _______________	Amerikanischer Ureinwohner oder **Indianer**
________ is often fed to animals.	Oft füttert man Tiere mit **Mais.**
__________ is a big orange vegetable.	Ein **Kürbis** ist ein großes orangefarbenes Gemüse.
Green __________ are my favourite vegetable.	Grüne **Bohnen** sind mein Lieblingsgemüse.
The _____________ wanted a new life in America.	Die **Siedler** wollten ein neues Leben in Amerika.
Plymouth was an early English _____________ .	Plymouth war eine frühe englische **Kolonie.**

1 Last letter – first letter

Der letzte Buchstabe von jedem Wort ist gleichzeitig der erste des nächsten Wortes.

1 Puppe
2 Leiter
3 gläubig
4 Rauch
5 außergewöhnlich
6 gähnen
7 edel
8 aufregend
9 Ziege
10 Truthahn
11 jung
12 Handschuhe
13 Frühling
14 Tor
15 Lippe

New words ▸ p. 38

A __________ shows important dates in history.	Ein **Zeitstrahl** zeigt wichtige Daten der Geschichte.
The __________________ for 'somebody' is *sb.*	Die **Abkürzung** für ‚somebody' ist *sb.*
Julius Cesar came to England in 55 ________ .	Julius Caesar kam 55 **v. Chr.** nach England.
45 AD = 45 years after __________ was born	45 AD = 45 Jahre nachdem **Christus** geboren wurde
Do you know who wrote ________ *of the Rings*?	Weißt du, wer ***Herr** der Ringe* geschrieben hat?
What's the date and place of your __________ ?	Was ist Ihr **Geburts**datum und -ort?
__________________ produces the food we eat.	Die **Landwirtschaft** produziert unsere Lebensmittel.
The fire ________ quickly because of the wind.	Das Feuer **verbreitete** sich schnell wegen des Windes.
compare _______________ pop with 60s pop	**heutigen** Pop mit Popmusik der 60er vergleichen
The area is too dry to __________ tomatoes.	Das Gebiet ist zu trocken um Tomaten **anzubauen**.
Columbus _____________ to America in 1492.	1492 **segelte** Columbus nach Amerika.
The _____________ came to America in 1620.	Die **Pilger** kamen im Jahr 1620 nach Amerika.
How did you _____________ your birthday?	Wie hast du deinen Geburtstag **gefeiert**?
the _______________ of the Queen's birthday	die **Feier** des Geburtstages der Königin
Farmers are very busy during the __________ .	Bauern sind während der **Ernte** sehr beschäftigt.
Are we __________ more clever than animals?	Sind wir **Menschen** klüger als Tiere?
This town was ____________ in the 11th century.	Diese Stadt wurde im 11. Jahrhundert **gegründet**.
Have they found out the __________ of the fire?	Haben sie die Brand**ursache** gefunden?
Why do football fans often __________ trouble?	Warum **verursachen** Fußballfans oft Ärger?
What's the ________ of cold weather on plants?	Welche **Wirkung** hat kaltes Wetter auf Pflanzen?
Think of the ________________ of your actions.	Bedenke die **Folgen** deiner Handlungen.
Is he the right person to __________ the group?	Ist er die richtige Person um die Gruppe zu **führen**?
The _____________ founded a new colony.	Die **Siedler** gründeten eine neue Kolonie.
The Thanksgiving __________ moved on slowly.	Der Erntedank**umzug** bewegte sich langsam voran.

2 Word search

Finde Wörter im Rätsel, um die Wortgruppen zu vervollständigen. (↓ →)

H	O	U	R	M	I	B	A	C	O	N	U	S	W	E	X	M
W	N	O	Y	T	C	J	C	H	I	L	D	P	P	D	X	A
W	I	N	D	O	W	Q	A	I	I	I	B	W	O	M	A	N
N	O	I	S	M	P	S	K	C	A	R	R	O	T	X	D	C
D	N	U	Y	A	J	A	Y	K	D	L	O	J	A	T	O	R
B	U	L	E	T	T	U	C	E	U	F	O	E	T	R	O	F
U	D	W	R	O	S	S	T	N	L	C	F	L	O	O	R	X
P	A	S	T	E	A	A	S	L	T	G	J	N	V	I	R	B
K	Y	V	U	X	A	G	D	S	T	E	A	K	B	A	L	A
H	G	P	R	E	S	E	N	T	G	N	F	B	V	W	G	P
R	L	B	K	W	Q	Q	V	A	B	F	Q	B	E	A	N	U
Y	R	P	E	N	U	G	M	I	N	U	T	E	F	L	Y	B
F	O	F	Y	E	A	R	L	R	D	T	T	E	H	L	T	A
U	O	S	B	S	S	H	T	S	V	U	W	F	L	N	J	B
Y	M	O	N	T	H	A	Q	B	T	R	L	A	O	U	G	Y
Y	O	R	T	H	H	A	A	T	E	E	N	A	G	E	R	U

vegetables

bean

meat

turkey

house

door

time

day

humans

man

New words ▸ p. 39

talk about politics in a ________________ class	Politik in einer **Sozialkunde**stunde besprechen
You're late. Take a taxi ______________ a bus.	Du bist spät dran. Nimm ein Taxi **statt** einem Bus.
The French ________________ began in 1789.	Die Französische **Revolution** begann 1789.
The US school year has two ______________ .	Das US-Schuljahr hat zwei **Semester**.
Please don't ______________ while I'm talking.	Bitte **unterbrich** nicht, wenn ich spreche.
have different ______________ on a topic	verschiedene **Meinungen** zu einem Thema haben
Please ____________ the cake with everyone else.	Bitte **teile** den Kuchen mit allen anderen.
What do we have next ____________ ? – Maths!	Was haben wir in der nächsten **Stunde**? – Mathe!
It was his ____________ that we were late.	Es war sein **Fehler**, dass wir zu spät waren.
You're so noisy. Can't you ______________ ?	Du bist so laut! Kannst du nicht **leise sein**?
a dangerous, but not ____________ , situation	eine gefährliche, aber nicht **hoffnungslose** Situation
She kissed him and _______ him a _______ .	Sie küsste und **umarmte** ihn.
A big _________ and kisses to Jo and Jake!	Eine dicke **Umarmung** und Küsse an Jo und Jake!

3 Hidden words

Ergänze die Wortgruppen, indem du Wörter mit Buchstaben des Wortes „celebration" bildest.

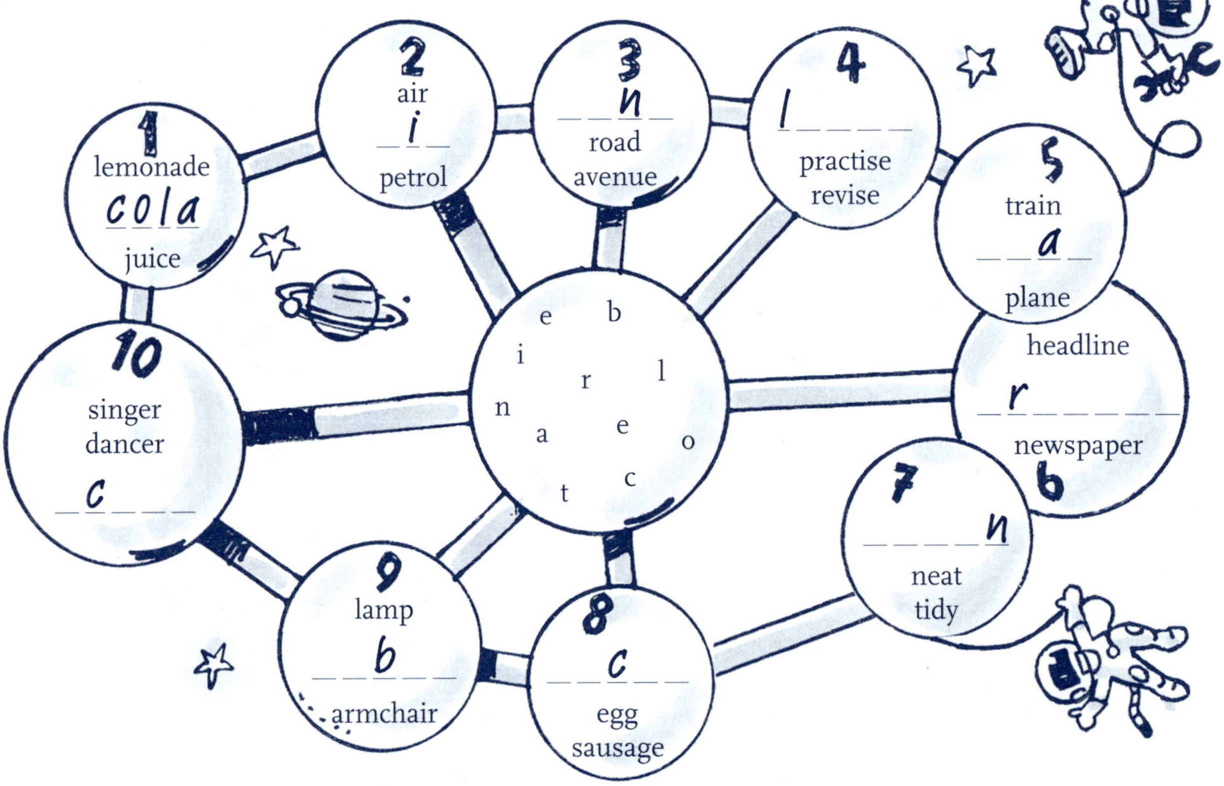

4 More about ... Traditional Native Americans homes

Vervollständige den Text mit den Wörtern aus der Box.

by called could enough kinds open possible skill themselves took

There are different ____________ (1) of Native American homes in different parts of North America, but the one we know best is usually ____________ (2) a wigwam in English. Building a wigwam was an important job, a ____________ (3) that had to be learned. This work, which usually ____________ (4) about three days, was often done ____________ (5) women, who used the wood from the forests near where the tribe lived. As a rule, wigwams were light structures, so that they ____________ (6) be moved easily if the tribe changed to another location. They were large ____________ (7) for about ten people. In the centre of each wigwam, there was a place for a fire. Here it was ____________ (8) to cook, or people could just keep ____________ (9) warm. The fire also gave them light and, above it, the wigwam was ____________ (10), so that the smoke could get out. Even in cold weather, wigwams were warm and comfortable places.

5 Lost words

Ergänze die Sätze mit den Wörtern rechts.

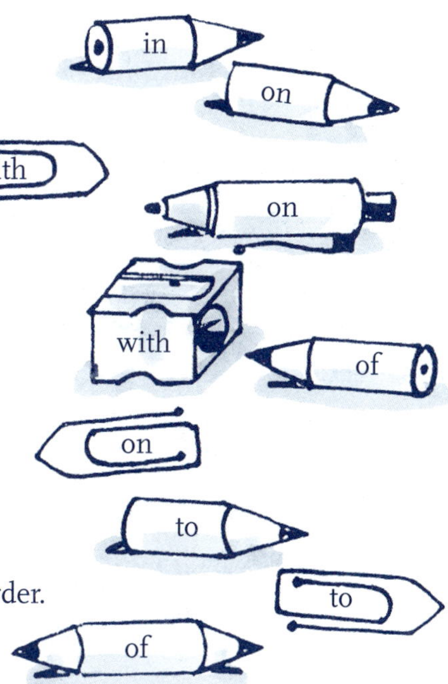

1 I hope you'll come up ____________ some good ideas!

2 Maybe I can meet you. It depends ____________ the time.

3 Does this street lead ____________ the station?

4 The rain in August had a bad effect ____________ the harvest.

5 We always have different opinions ____________ this topic.

6 Thank you for sharing your ideas ____________ us.

7 Cut out these pictures and put them ____________ the right order.

8 What line ____________ work is your dad in?

9 Everyone looks up ____________ Jake because he does so much for the team.

10 The police are still trying to discover the cause ____________ the accident.

New words ▸ *pp. 40–41*

an Indian village in a ______________ museum	ein indianisches Dorf in einem **Freilicht**museum
How many teachers are there on the _________ ?	Wie viele Lehrer gibt es im **Lehrerkollegium**?
All ________________ will have to work longer.	Alle **Mitarbeiter** werden länger arbeiten müssen.
_________ warmly today. It's very cold outside.	**Zieh dich** heute warm **an**! Es ist kalt draußen.
Please ____________ on the baby while I'm out.	Bitte **pass auf** das Baby auf, während ich weg bin.
Crazy Horse was a _________ of the Sioux.	Crazy Horse war ein **Häuptling** der Sioux.
a pop-art __________________ at the museum	eine Pop-Art **Ausstellung** im Museum
It may hurt a bit, so try to be _________ .	Es könnte weh tun, also versuche **tapfer** zu sein.
The vegetables grow very well in this _________ .	Das Gemüse wächst sehr gut auf diesem **Boden**.
The _________ showed us all the sights.	Der **Reiseleiter** zeigte uns alle Sehenswürdigkeiten.
Do you know ___________ Jo's at home?	Weißt du, **ob** Jo zu Hause ist?
Thanks. Your tips were very ___________ to me.	Danke! Deine Tipps waren sehr **hilfreich** für mich.

6 Word families

a) Finde die passenden Verben zu den angegebenen Nomen.

1 shot – shoot
2 celebration – ___________
3 cause – ___________
4 speech – ___________
5 revision – ___________
6 filling – ___________
7 taste – ___________
8 death – ___________
9 immigration – ___________
10 collection – ___________
11 sale – ___________
12 comparison – ___________

b) Vervollständige die Sätze mit einem Nomen oder einem Verb aus der Liste in a).

1 The firemen still don't know the cause of the fire.
2 Sorry, I can't come to your party. I have to ___________ for my test.
3 The whole country was shocked by the King's early ___________ .
4 When do you _____________ Mother's Day in England?
5 The president is going to make a ___________ to the nation tomorrow.

New words ▸ p. 42

Everything was as ______ . Nothing was different.	Alles war wie **üblich**. Es gab keine Veränderungen.
It's a ____________ to play tricks on April 1st.	Es ist **Tradition**, am 1. April Streiche zu spielen.
There was live ________________ at the party.	Auf der Party gab es Live-**Unterhaltung**.
My brother studies history and ___________ .	Mein Bruder studiert Geschichte und **Politik**.
Please do exercises 1 and 2 on the _________ .	Macht bitte Übungen 1 und 2 auf dem **Arbeitsblatt**.
This book is a useful _________ of information.	Dieses Buch ist eine nützliche Informations**quelle**.

7 Crossword

Across

3 a big bird that Americans eat at Thanksgiving (6)
6 what plants grow in (4)
7 bow and ★ (5)
8 How do you ★ the New Year in Germany? (9)
9 a public event where you can see paintings or other works of art (10)
12 sb. who travels to a place for religious reasons (7)
13 Your ★ is what you think about something. (7)
15 Rain has had a bad ★ on the tourist industry. (6)
18 The US ★ industry produces a lot of food for the home market. (7)
20 Please blow out the ★ before you go out. (6)
21 a farm animal that gives milk, but not a cow (6)

Down

1 not afraid in dangerous situations (5)
2 Over 30 different bands took part in the ★ through the city centre. (5)
4 There will be music, dancing, films and other kinds of ★ . (13)
5 Your date of ★ is the day you were born. (5)
10 something that a fire produces, and which goes up into the air (5)
11 Please don't ★ me while I'm speaking. (9)
14 The news ★ quickly through the village. (6)
16 an important religious book (5)
17 sb. who shows a city to tourists (5)
19 Sue gave her dad a ★ and a big kiss. (3)

New words ▸ pp. 45–51

The same __________ every day! Nothing changes.	Jeden Tag dieselbe **Routine**! Nichts ändert sich.
Can you __________ the milk from the kitchen?	Kannst du die Milch aus der Küche **holen**?
Cows must be __________ twice a day.	Kühe müssen zweimal täglich **gemolken** werden.
'Hands up, or I'll __________', said the robber.	„Hände hoch oder ich **schieße**," sagte der Räuber.
She went into the church and said a __________ .	Sie ging in die Kirche hinein und sprach ein **Gebet**.
In a church, you can sing and __________ .	In einer Kirche kann man singen und **beten**.
It's a __________ , so please don't tell anyone.	Es ist ein **Geheimnis**, also bitte sag es niemandem.
Please keep it __________ . Don't tell anyone.	Bitte halte es **geheim**. Sag es niemandem.
Please learn the first two __________ of the poem.	Bitte lernt die ersten zwei **Strophen** des Gedichts.
Aids is a terrible __________ .	AIDS ist eine schreckliche **Krankheit**.
The __________ of the castle is at 3 pm.	Die **Führung** durch das Schloss ist um drei.
Read the heading and __________ .	Lies die Überschrift und **Zwischenüberschriften**.
Thousands came to the __________ against the war.	Tausende kamen zum **Protest** gegen den Krieg.
Be __________ . Say exactly what you saw.	Sei **spezifisch**. Sag genau, was du gesehen hast.

8 Hour glasses

Übersetze die Wörter und trage sie in die passende Sanduhr ein.

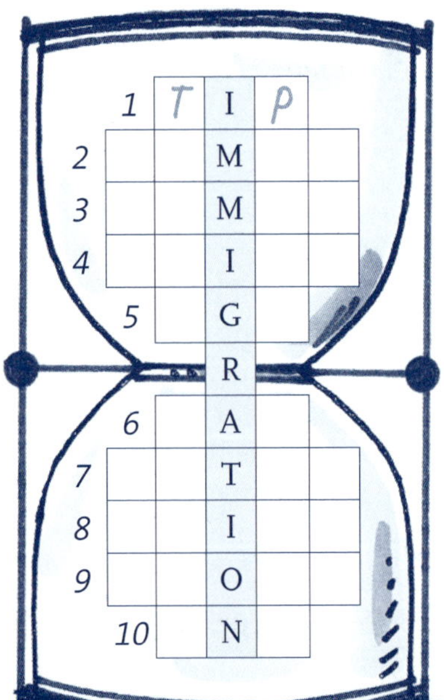

1 aufführen – Spitze
2 Spiele – Rauch
3 Mensch –Zaun
4 verschwenden – Häuptling
5 Alter – besorgen
6 Nuss – Benzin (AE)
7 nachdem – Schlange, Reihe
8 letzte(r,s) – Heilige(r)
9 schöner – (er)schießen
10 Schlüssel – und

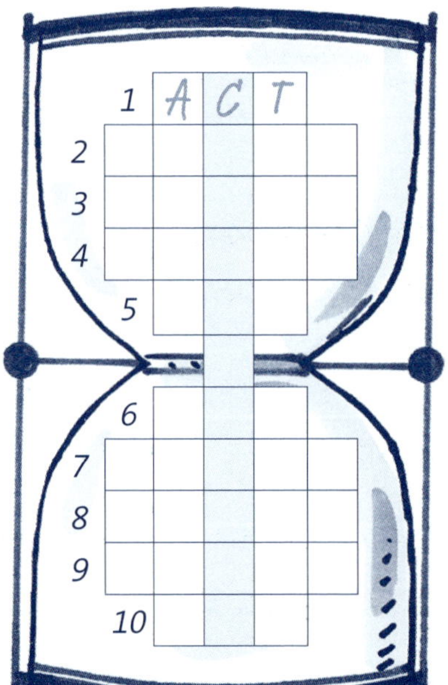

Das geheime Wort heißt: *Englisch* __________

Deutsch __________

9 Spot the mistakes

In jedem Satz sind zwei Fehler. Unterstreiche und korrigiere sie.

1 Change the <u>tableclothe</u> before you ley the table, please. tablecloth ______
2 Maiz can be used to food farm animals. ______ ______
3 Have you read the latest report on the effekts of smokeing? ______ ______
4 Please don't interupt other students wile they're speaking. ______ ______
5 Can you read the first vers of the peom, please. ______ ______
6 Contact a member of staf if you have a spezific problem. ______ ______

10 The best word

Finde in jeder Schublade das Wort, das am besten in die Lücke passt.

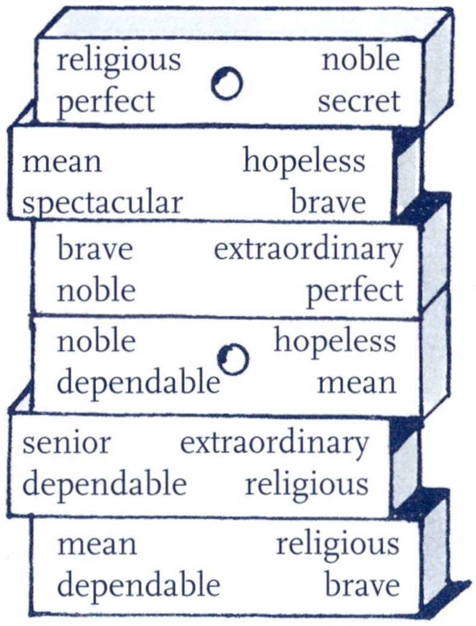

1 This is ______, so don't tell anyone.
2 The view from the Empire State Building is quite ______.
3 What great weather! It's the ______ day for a picnic.
4 What? Jake's late again? He really is just ______.
5 I can't believe it! That really is a(n) ______ story.
6 It's really ______ to call somebody names.

11 Odd word out

Ein Wort passt nicht. Finde und unterstreiche es.

1 arrow – ruler – rubber – sharpener
2 apple – banana – maize – strawberry
3 beans – onions – potatoes – turkey
4 cow – goat – hedgehog – sheep
5 line – paragraph – staff – verse
6 candle – harvest – lamp – light
7 drive – fly – sail – sale
8 fault – hug – kiss – smile
9 brave – lonely – sad – unhappy
10 dependable – friendly – helpful – rude
11 engineer – firefighter – settler – teacher
12 coast – colony – island – mountain

New words ▸ p. 52

The pirates always drank in the same ________ .	Die Piraten tranken immer in derselben **Schenke.**
You sometimes ask ________ silly questions!	Du stellst manchmal **verdammt** dumme Fragen!
A ______________ usually wears a uniform.	Ein **Soldat** trägt meistens Uniform.
Cats ________ mice, and usually catch them.	Katzen **jagen** Mäuse und erwischen sie meistens.
____________ seeing the film? – Yes, it's great!	**Lohnt es sich,** den Film anzusehen? – Ja, er ist toll!
a ________ against smoking in restaurants	ein **Gesetz** gegen das Rauchen in Restaurants
It's _________________ to sell state secrets.	Es ist **Hochverrat**, Staatsgeheimnisse zu verkaufen.
Is the king popular with all his ______________ ?	Ist der König bei all seinen **Untertanen** beliebt?
Who led the ______________ against the king?	Wer hat den **Aufstand** gegen den König angeführt?
We celebrated our team's 1–0 ______________ .	Wir feierten den 1:0-**Sieg** unserer Mannschaft.
____________________ ! I don't want to see you.	**Geh mir aus den Augen!** Ich will dich nicht sehen.

12 Definitions

Vervollständige die Definitionen mit Wörtern aus der linken Sprühwolke. Trage die Lösungen aus der anderen Sprühwolke in die rechte Spalte ein.

1	put your *arms* around someone and __________ them	*hug*
2	a thing children __________ with that looks like a __________ or small person	____________
3	a place where water comes ________ from under the ________________	____________
4	have ________________ at a birthday or other special __________	____________
5	people who go to a ________ country or ___________ to live there	____________
6	people who ________ for a company or at a ________________	____________

13 Words with the same meaning

Finde in der Box Wörter, die dieselbe Bedeutung haben wie die fettgedruckten Wörter.
Trage sie ein und schreibe die deutsche Übersetzung auf.

apartment difficult kind near
scared supporters topic ~~trip~~

1 Have a good **journey**/ trip ! See you when you're back. Reise

2 We're looking for a holiday **flat** / ________________ on the coast. ________________

3 We live quite **close to** / ________________ a tube station. ________________

4 I've found a really interesting **subject** / ________________ for my essay. ________________

5 There's a big crowd of ManU **fans** / ________________ in the stadium. ________________

6 What **sort** / ________________ of food do you normally eat? ________________

7 Did you know that Jake is **afraid** / ________________ of mice? ________________

8 Did you find the exercise **hard** / ________________ ? ________________

14 Word ladder

Gehe von unten nach oben, indem du auf jeder Sprosse einen Buchstaben veränderst.

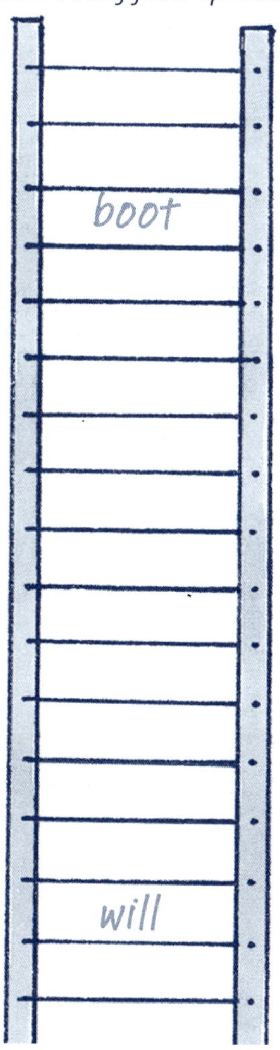

We have lots of sheep, but only one ★.

The next ★ for Orkney leaves at 16.29.

Does this football ★ belong to you?

Frank is quite tall – over six ★.

Is there enough ★ and drink for everyone?

It wasn't a very ★ idea to go out without a jacket.

Are your earrings made of real ★ ?

Can you ★ these bags while I look for my keys?

The horses escaped through a ★ in the fence.

A ★ can move about five kilos of soil in 20 minutes.

We live about a ★ from the nearest village.

He gets up early every morning to ★ the cows.

Do you prefer ★ or spicy dishes?

You'll need to be careful of the ★ animals.

Who do you think ★ win the final?

Can you ★ the bottle with water please?

New words ▸ p. 53

The murderer spent 15 years in ________ .	Der Mörder verbrachte 15 Jahre im **Gefängnis.**
A ____________ has escaped from prison.	Ein **Gefangener** ist aus dem Gefängnis entflohen.
She's a soldier in the American ___________ .	Sie ist Soldatin in der amerikanischen **Armee.**
Killing somebody is a serious ______________ .	Jemanden zu töten ist ein schweres **Verbrechen.**
What crimes did the prisoner ________________ ?	Welche Verbrechen hat die Gefangene **begangen**?
______________ someone to three years in prison	jemanden zu drei Jahren Gefängnis **verurteilen**
a life ___________________ for murder	eine lebenslängliche **Haftstrafe** wegen Mord
The president can ______________ the prisoners.	Der Präsident kann die Gefangenen **begnadigen.**
The ___________ took place in the prison at 6 am.	Die **Hinrichtung** fand um 6 Uhr im Gefängnis statt.
Don't be afraid. You're ___________ friends here.	Hab keine Angst. Du bist hier **unter** Freunden.
The bankrobber __________ the money in a field.	Der Bankräuber **vergrub** das Geld auf einem Feld.
We don't know if he's dead or ______________ .	Wir wissen nicht, ob er tot oder **am Leben** ist.
If you ___________ the sofa I'll look under it.	Wenn du das Sofa an**hebst**, gucke ich darunter.
3 feet = 1 ___________ (= 0.9144 metres)	3 Fuß = 1 **Yard** (= 0,9144 Meter)
He lived alone in a little _____ in the mountains.	Er lebte allein in einer kleinen **Hütte** in den Bergen.
She sat at her desk ________________ by books.	Sie saß am Schreibtisch von Büchern **umgeben.**
A ___________ stood in front of the castle gate.	Ein **Wachposten** stand vor dem Tor zum Schloss.
The sudden attack caused great ______________ .	Der plötzliche Angriff stiftete große **Verwirrung.**
Don't ask so many questions! It ___________ me.	Stell nicht so viele Fragen! Es **verwirrt** mich.
I've seen this film ________________ times.	Ich habe diesen Film **mehrere** Male gesehen.
Have they found the ________ the murderer used?	Haben sie the **Schusswaffe** des Mörders gefunden?
Without air you can't ______________ .	Ohne Luft kann man nicht **atmen.**
___________ the bottle before you drink the juice.	**Schüttle** die Flasche, bevor du den Saft trinkst.
The children ___________________ up the steps.	Die Kinder **stürmten** die Treppe hinauf.
A light ______________ suddenly in the night sky.	Ein Licht **leuchtete** plötzlich am Nachthimmel.
Was anybody killed when the bomb ___________ ?	Wurde jemand getötet, als die Bombe **explodierte**?

New words ▸ p. 54

Long discussions are often a __________ of time.	Lange Diskussionen sind oft Zeit**verschwendung**.
If your nose ______________ again, lie down.	Wenn deine Nase wieder **blutet**, leg dich hin.
Two horses were needed to pull the __________ .	Man brauchte zwei Pferde um den **Karren** zu ziehen.
The robbers __________ their victim to a chair.	Die Räuber **banden** ihr Opfer an einem Stuhl **fest**.
We tied his hands together with a ___________ .	Wir banden seine Hände mit einem **Seil** zusammen.
Giraffes have very long _____________ .	Giraffen haben sehr lange Hälse.
He's the _____________ at the village church.	Er ist der **Pastor** an der Dorfkirche.
When she saw the rat she _____________ loudly.	Als sie die Ratte sah, **schrie** sie laut.
How can I ever pay back these ___________ ?	Wie kann ich jemals diese **Schulden** zurückzahlen?
Why do you _____________ telling old jokes?	Warum erzählst du **ständig** alte Witze?
Finally she _________________________ her aim.	Endlich **erreichte** sie ihr Ziel.

15 Word pairs

Welche Wörter passen zusammen?

16 Pronunciation

Ordne die Wörter aus der Box der richtigen Aussprachegruppe zu.

colonist colony commit consequence doll grow hopeless opinion period politics protest revolution rope shot smoke soldier tablecloth victory

ə	ɒ	əʊ
revolution	politics	grow

17 Word friends

In jedem Haus gibt es drei Wörter bzw. Wortverbindungen, die man direkt nach dem Verb auf der Fahne benutzen kann. Unterstreiche sie.

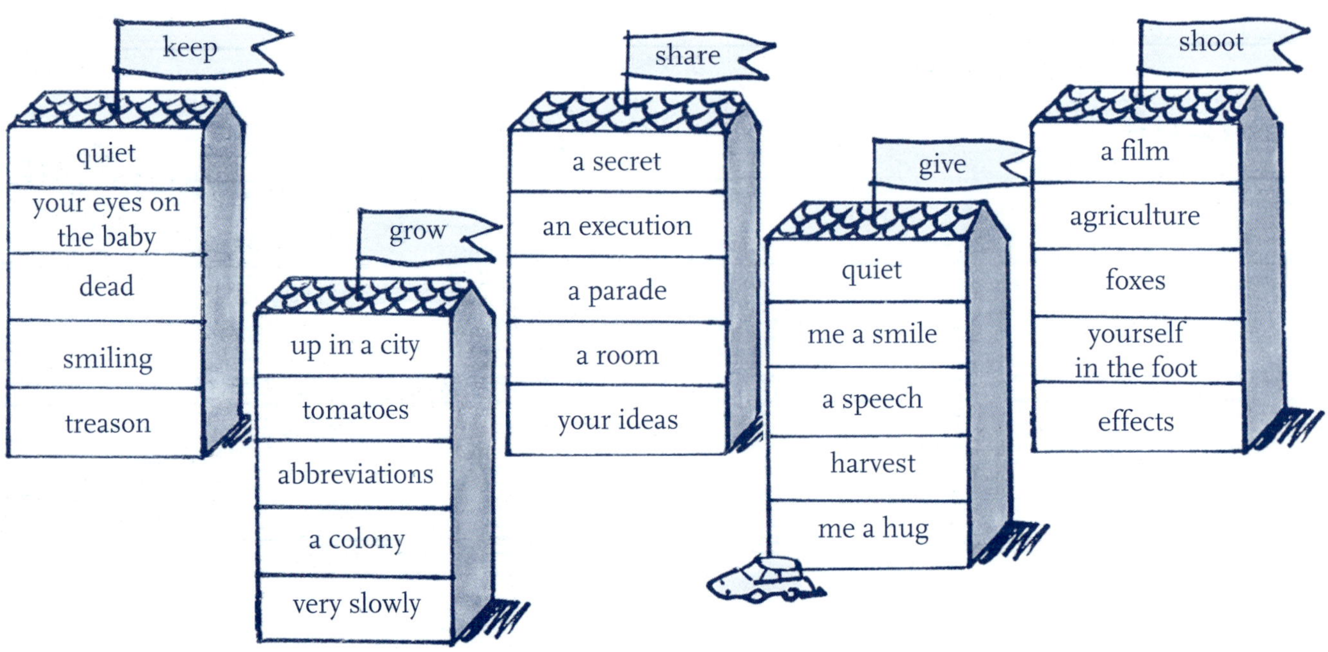

New words ▸ *p. 56*

A good ________________ can explain a picture.	Eine gute **Bildunterschrift** kann ein Bild erklären.
He was ________________ before he was president.	Er war **Gouverneur**, bevor er Präsident wurde.
________________ are often badly paid.	**Wanderarbeiter** werden oft schlecht bezahlt.
________________ kids often sleep under bridges.	**Obdachlose** Kinder schlafen oft unter Brücken.
He stopped to ______________ the view.	Er hielt an, um die Aussicht zu **bewundern.**
A ______________ person has lots of great ideas.	Ein **kreativer** Mensch hat viele tolle Ideen.
the latest ________________ from the IT world	die neuesten **Innovationen** aus der Welt der IT
High ______________ hit the cliffs.	Hohe **Wellen** schlugen gegen die Felsen.
Many houses were destroyed by ______________ .	Viele Häuser wurden vom **Waldbrand** zerstört.
Fires are also a danger for ______________ .	Brände sind auch eine Gefahr für die **Tierwelt**.

1 Words with different meanings

Finde in der Liste die passenden Wörter zu den Paaren 1–8.
Trage sie ein und unterstreiche die deutschen Entsprechungen.

spring
subject
wave
put
~~right~~
counter
mean
lift

1
a) Diese Antwort ist richtig.
b) Gleich musst du rechts abbiegen.
right

2
a) Was bedeutet dieser Satz?
b) Sei nicht immer so gemein zu mir.
____

3
a) Diese Blumen blühen im Frühling.
b) Wasser aus einer Quelle trinken
____

4
a) Er steht jeden Tag hinter der Theke.
b) den Spielstein ein Feld weiter bewegen
____

5
a) Kannst du bitte den Stuhl hochheben?
b) den Fahrstuhl ins 12. Stockwerk nehmen
____

6
a) Die Kinder spielten in den Wellen.
b) Winke, damit ich dich sehen kann.
____

7
a) Kannst du es anders formulieren?
b) Wo kann ich die Bücher hinlegen?
____

8
a) Englisch ist ihr Lieblingsfach.
b) Ihr Vater ist britischer Staatsangehöriger.
____

New words ▸ p. 58

A __________ of kids prefer TV to radio.	Eine **Mehrheit** der Kinder zieht TV dem Radio vor.
A small __________ were against the new law.	Eine kleine **Minderheit** war gegen das neue Gesetz.
We have ________ rain forests than 50 years ago.	Wir haben **weniger** Regenwälder als vor 50 Jahren.
She has a positive __________ towards work.	Sie hat eine positive **Einstellung** zur Arbeit.
He made some helpful __________ on my plan.	Er machte nützliche **Kommentare** zu meinem Plan.
This machine never works! It's __________ !	Diese Maschine funktioniert nie! Sie ist **nutzlos**!
A good __________ prepares you for life.	Eine gute **Erziehung** bereitet auf das Leben vor.
An A is the highest __________ you can get.	Ein A ist die beste **Note**, die man bekommen kann.
He's __________ against minorities.	Er ist **voreingenommen** gegenüber Minderheiten.
Religious __________ is still a problem.	Religiöse **Vorurteile** sind immer noch ein Problem.
The old laws __________ against women.	Die alten Gesetze **diskriminieren** Frauen.
End __________ against minorities!	Beendet **Diskriminierung** gegenüber Minderheiten!
The ________ of old paintings is going up again.	Der **Wert** von alten Gemälden steigt wieder.
Is it an __________ to have rich parents?	Ist es ein **Vorteil**, reiche Eltern zu haben?
discuss advantages and __________	Vor- und **Nachteile** diskutieren
We use a __________ dictionary.	Wir benutzen ein **zweisprachiges** Wörterbuch.
It's difficult to __________ without you.	Es ist schwierig, ohne dich **zurechtzukommen**.
Many Mexicans enter the USA __________ ly.	Viele Mexikaner reisen **illegal** in die USA ein.
It's perfectly __________ to copy your own CDs.	Es ist vollkommen **legal**, eigene CDs zu kopieren.
You have to work hard to __________ .	Du musst hart arbeiten, um **Erfolg** zu **haben**.
There are good __________ between the states.	Es gibt gute **Beziehungen** zwischen den Staaten.

2 The fourth word

Welches Wort fehlt hier?

1 UK – queen	US – __________	*4* more – majority	fewer – __________
2 good – advantage	bad – __________	*5* hope – hopeless	home – __________
3 right – legal	wrong – __________	*6* translate – translation	educate – __________

3 Word groups

Trage die Wörter von der Wiese in die richtigen Kletterseile ein.

~~box office~~ – cattle – chicken – cliff – college – computer – cow – crash – ~~crime film~~ – director – discrimination – documentary – download – e-mail – ~~ethnic group~~ – goat – grade – happy ending – harbour – ~~high school~~ – horse – immigrant – majority – minority – monitor – movie – online forum – population – prejudice – rock – scene – sea – segregation – semester – sheep – software – student – teacher – term – test – tide – turkey – waves – webcam – website

New words ▸ p. 59

I have a written __________ for math.	Ich habe eine schriftliche **Hausaufgabe** für Mathe.
What's the big __________ with red flowers called?	Wie heißt die große **Pflanze** mit den roten Blüten?
I'd like to __________ new flowers in the garden.	Ich möchte neue Blumen im Garten **pflanzen.**
They always __________ graffiti on this wall!	Sie **sprayen** immer Graffiti an diese Wand!
Water __________ about 70 per cent of the earth.	Wasser **bedeckt** etwa 70 Prozent der Erde.
Are the seats made of leather or __________ ?	Sind die Sitze aus Leder oder **Kunststoff**?
A hat __________ you from the sun.	Ein Hut **schützt** dich vor der Sonne.
Spiders have 8 legs; __________ only have 6.	Spinnen haben 8 Beine, **Insekten** haben nur 6.
He's doing __________ research on frogs.	Er macht **biologische** Forschung zu Fröschen.
This is a new __________ of learning languages.	Dies ist eine neue **Methode**, Sprachen zu lernen.
We must try to spend __________ money.	Wir müssen versuchen, **weniger** Geld auszugeben.
You have to __________ strawberries by hand.	Man muss Erdbeeren mit den Händen **pflücken.**
Have you got any __________ on the subject?	Hast du ein paar **Gedanken** zum Thema?
__________ usually has more sugar than juice.	**Limonade** enthält meistens mehr Zucker als Saft.

4 Word ladder

Gehe von unten nach oben, indem du auf jeder Sprosse einen Buchstaben veränderst.

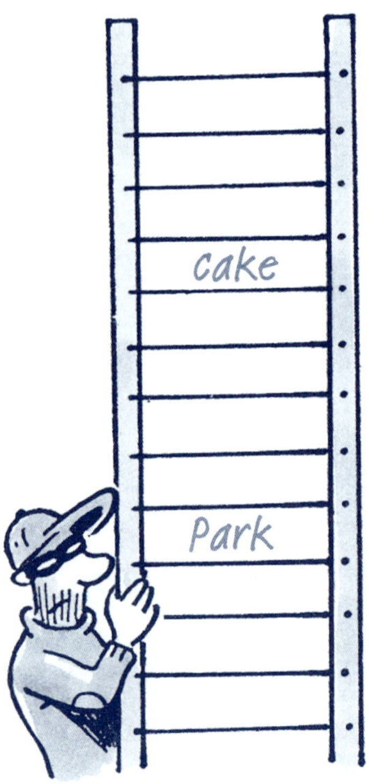

Jake's mum is going to ★ another baby.
A huge ★ came towards the beach.
Can you ★ me up at 6 o'clock, please?
Mum made a chocolate ★ for my birthday.
'A very interesting ★,' the detective thought.
Who's taking ★ of your cat when you're away?
We'll need two horses to pull this ★ .
I was late at the cinema so I missed the first ★ of the film.
There's an open-air pop concert tonight in Central ★.
Why didn't the dog ★ when the thieves came?
The sun disappeared behind the ★ clouds.
I hope I'll get a good ★ in English.

5 Number crossword

Gleiche Zahlen sind gleiche Buchstaben.
Die angegebenen Lösungen helfen dir,
das gesamte Rätsel zu lösen.
Alle Wörter sind in dieser Unit neu.

Wo im Rätsel findet man das englische Wort für …

bewundern f down

Vorteil ______

Erfolg haben ______

Wert ______

Methode ______

pflanzen ______

zudecken ______

legal ______

6 Word search

Finde 20 Begriffe aus dem Wortfeld „travel and tourism". (↓ →)
Schreibe sie auf und übersetze sie ins Deutsche.

I	A	T	R	A	I	N	S	B	S	P	N	U	G
N	T	T	R	Z	H	O	L	I	D	A	Y	S	E
F	T	U	M	H	O	T	R	K	K	C	Q	J	M
O	R	X	A	O	O	O	R	J	O	K	P	O	C
R	A	R	P	T	Z	U	L	Y	H	N	L	U	A
M	C	E	A	E	C	R	I	Y	D	U	A	R	R
A	T	S	T	L	S	I	G	H	T	S	N	N	A
T	I	T	T	M	U	S	E	U	M	T	E	E	V
I	O	A	Z	T	E	T	R	T	R	I	P	Y	A
O	N	U	B	I	H	T	P	T	E	N	T	O	N
N	H	R	C	C	P	A	S	S	E	N	G	E	R
O	X	A	A	K	L	S	O	U	V	E	N	I	R
L	C	N	M	E	W	G	C	W	I	U	A	Q	Q
G	T	T	P	T	N	Y	N	N	Q	O	Z	J	T

train – Zug

New words ▸ p. 60

an expensive area with many __________ families	eine teure Gegend mit vielen **reichen** Familien
The country's ______________ depends on oil.	Der **Reichtum** des Landes hängt vom Öl ab.
We usually eat ______________ at about 7 pm.	Wir essen meistens um sieben **Abendbrot**.
The border _____ from San Diego to Brownsville.	Die Grenze **verläuft** von San Diego bis Brownsville.
He dropped a glass. __________ , it didn't break.	Er ließ ein Glas fallen. Es ging **jedoch** nicht kaputt.
The thief noticed two policemen on __________ .	Der Dieb bemerkte zwei Polizisten auf Streife.
The Sahara is a __________ in Africa.	Die Sahara ist eine **Wüste** in Afrika.
She fell into the river and ____________ .	Sie fiel in den Fluss und **ertrank**.
____________ ! Do not touch this fence!	**Warnung**! Diesen Zaun nicht berühren!
We were ______________ not to swim here.	Man hat uns davor **gewarnt**, hier zu schwimmen.

7 Odd word out

Ein Wort passt nicht. Finde und unterstreiche es.

1 minister – governor – coach – president

2 wildlife – waves – beach – rocks

3 comment – report – article – monitor

4 jacket – scarf – cap – caption

5 shout – scream – shake – cry

6 breakfast – lunch – soda – supper

7 creative – intelligent – clever – plain

8 attitude – advantage – view – opinion

9 get along – win – lose – succeed

10 tease – neck – throat – shoulder

8 Word families

Finde die passenden Nomen zu den angegebenen Verben.

1 warn – warning

2 confuse – ______________

3 think – ______________

4 plant – ______________

5 succeed – ______________

6 discriminate – ______________

7 bleed – ______________

8 waste – ______________

9 own – ______________

10 pray – ______________

11 sentence – ______________

12 hug – ______________

New words ▸ p. 61

The Pacific ________ is west of America.	Der Pazifische **Ozean** ist westlich von Amerika.
You'll find all the information in the ________ .	Du findest alle Informationen auf dem **Flugblatt.**
We can ________ the pizza to your house.	Wir können die Pizza ins Haus **liefern.**
Old factories cause a lot of ________ .	Alte Fabriken verursachen viel **Verschmutzung**.
Where does the Rhine ________ into the sea?	Wo **fließt** der Rhein ins Meer?
I tried to ________ him from stealing money.	Ich versuchte ihn davon **abhalten**, Geld zu stehlen.
The police are trying to ________ crime.	Die Polizei versucht, Verbrechen zu **verhindern.**
It's a ________ factory – the largest in Europe!	Es ist ein **Riesen**fabrik ist die größte Europas!
Buy a house! Become a ________ at last!	Kauft ein Haus! Werdet endlich **Eigenheimbesitzer!**
The ________ of the shop is a friend of mine.	Der **Eigentümer** des Ladens ist ein Freund von mir.
Rich people often ________ more than one house.	Reiche Leute **besitzen** oft mehr als ein Haus.
We must ________ the number of accidents.	Wir müssen die Zahl der Unfälle **reduzieren.**
Many ________ can cause disease.	Viele **Bakterien** können Krankheiten verursachen.
Does Germany need a better school ________ ?	Braucht Deutschland ein besseres Schul**system**?
________ problems like air pollution	**Umwelt**probleme wie Luftverschmutzung
How can we save our natural ________ ?	Wie können wir unsere natürliche **Umwelt** retten?

9 The best word

Finde in jeder Schublade das Wort, das am besten in die Lücke passt.

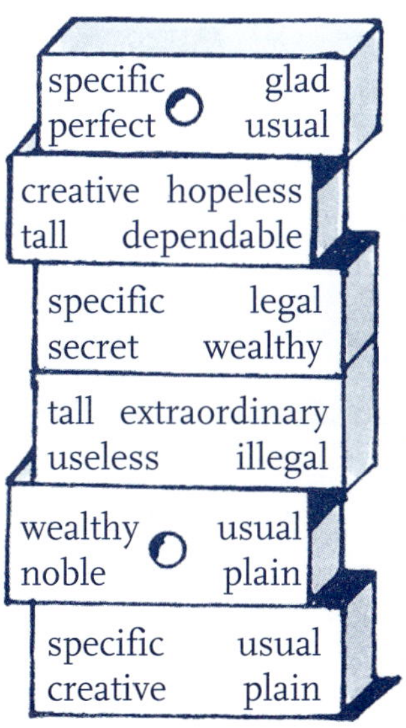

1 It's a ________ day for a picnic.

2 He's really ________ ! He never does anything right.

3 It's ________ , so don't tell anyone.

4 Do you know if it's ________ to copy CDs?

5 She's from a ________ family, although they're quite poor, really.

6 If you have a ________ problem, you can get help online.

New words ▸ pp. 64–71

"Awesome" is a ______ for great.	„Awesome" ist ein **Synonym** für great.
You're late! You ______ missed me.	Du bist zu spät! Du hättest mich **beinahe** verpasst.
Many ______ minorities live in London.	In London wohnen viele **ethnische** Minderheiten.
______ are words that go together.	**Kollokationen** sind Wörter, die zusammengehören.
Black is the ______ of white.	Schwarz ist das **Gegenteil** von weiß.
Pick the fruit before it gets too ______ .	Pflück das Obst, bevor es zu **reif** wird.
There's no alcohol in a ______ .	In einem **alkoholfreien Getränk** ist kein Alkohol.
write a ______ text about California	einen **Sach**text über Kalifornien schreiben
Use pictures to ______ your talk!	Benutze Bilder, um deinen Vortrag zu **illustrieren**!
He founded an ______ that helps animals.	Er gründete eine **Organisation**, die Tieren hilft.
An ______ helps you to plan an essay.	Eine **Übersicht** hilft dir, einen Aufsatz zu planen.

10 Hour glasses

Übersetze die Wörter und trage sie in die passende Sanduhr ein.

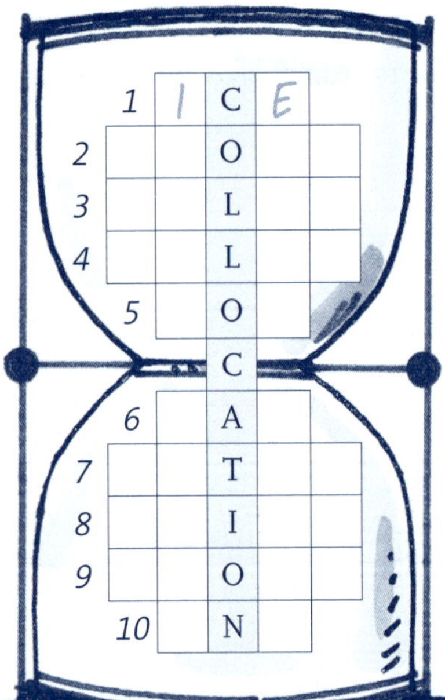

1 (an)nähen – Eis
2 zwischen – Eigentümer/in
3 Wert – zudecken
4 hügelig – (Auto)fahrt
5 probieren, kosten – Fuchs
6 Gesetz – beenden
7 holen – Begrenzung
8 Ozean – Fremdenführer/in
9 ertrinken – seit
10 aß – Schluss

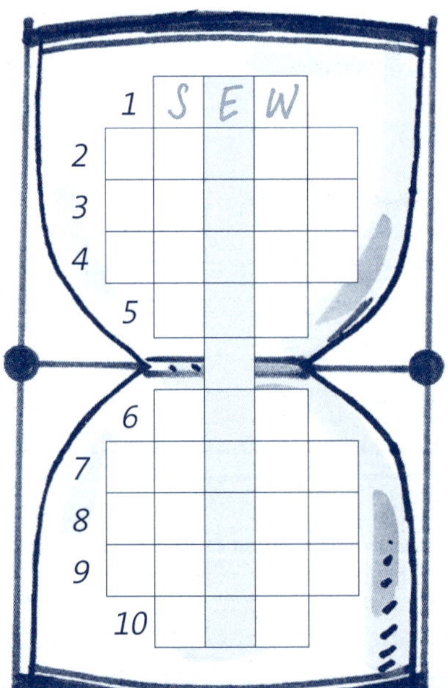

Das geheime Wort heißt: Englisch ______

Deutsch ______

New words ▸ p. 72

__________ are grown along the Mosel.	Entlang der Mosel werden **Weintrauben** angebaut.
This summer shirt is made of 100% __________ .	Dieses Sommerhemd ist aus 100% **Baumwolle**.
What __________ is the parcel? – About 7 kilos.	Welches **Gewicht** hat das Paket? – Ungefähr 7 Kilo.
The host __________ his guests warmly.	Der Gastgeber **begrüßte** seine Gäste freundlich.
We work every day __________ Sunday.	Wir arbeiten jeden Tag **außer** Sonntag.
Don't __________ coffee on your new shirt!	**Verschütte** keinen Kaffee auf dein neues Hemd!
There were no free __________ on the train.	Es gab keine freien **Plätze** im Zug.
Stop crying and __________ your tears.	**Wisch** dir die Tränen **ab** und hör auf zu weinen.
He wiped the __________ from his face.	Er wischte den **Schweiß** aus seinem Gesicht.
Your __________ is above your eyes and nose.	Die **Stirn** ist über den Augen und der Nase.
At __________ the sun disappears	Beim **Sonnenuntergang** verschwindet die Sonne
... and it appears again at __________ .	... und sie erscheint wieder beim **Sonnenaufgang**.
Lots of birds eat __________ .	Viele Vögel fresssen **Regenwürmer**.
__________ the floor before the guests arrive	den Boden **kehren**, bevor die Gäste ankommen
Grapes are grown in __________ .	Weintrauben werden in **Weinbergen** angebaut.
If oil prices __________ , petrol will cost more.	Wenn die Ölpreise **steigen**, wird Benzin teurer.

11 Verb forms

Ergänze die Tabelle der unregelmäßigen Verben.

1	keep	kept	kept
2		swept	
3	rise		
4	bleed		
5		grew	
6			led
7		cost	
8			felt

9	spread		
10		shook	
11			thrown
12			spoken
13		fell	
14	teach		
15	put		
16			made

New words ▸ pp. 73–74

Wipe your nose with a ________________ !	Wisch deine Nase mit einem **Taschentuch** ab!
We got good seats in the fifth __________ .	Wir haben gute Plätze in der 5. **Reihe** bekommen.
If you eat any more, you'll be ____________ .	Wenn du noch mehr isst, wird dir **schlecht**.
Please stand ____________ and don't move!	Bitte **ruhig** bleiben und nicht bewegen!
The books on the shelf are covered in __________ .	Die Bücher im Regal sind mit **Staub** bedeckt.
Where's the __________ ? The grass needs water.	Wo ist der **Schlauch?** Der Rasen braucht Wasser.
I can _______________ to new things quickly.	Ich kann mich schnell an Neues **gewöhnen.**
Our cat loves to __________ on my bed.	Unsere Katze liebt es, auf meinem Bett zu **liegen.**
The ____________ called all the teachers together.	Der **Schulleiter** rief alle Lehrer zusammen.
Where can I ____________ for this course?	Wo kann ich mich für diesen Kurs **einschreiben**?
The new student _______________ himself to us.	Der neue Schüler hat sich uns **vorgestellt.**
Could you ____________ me the salt, please?	Könnten Sie mir bitte das Salz **reichen**?
He's so rude! Can't he be more ____________ ?	Er ist so unhöflich! Kann er nicht **höflicher** sein?
Luckily I have ____________________ parents.	Zum Glück habe ich **verständnisvolle** Eltern.
____________ is always after the third period.	Die **Pause** ist immer nach der dritten Stunde.
Where's the _______________ in this restaurant?	Wo ist die **Toilette** in diesem Restaurant?
I often get ____________________ when it's cold.	Ich bekomme oft **Gänsehaut,** wenn's kalt ist.
A ____________ is somebody who tells stories.	Ein **Erzähler** ist jemand, der Geschichten erzählt.

12 Opposites

Trage die Gegenteile der fettgedruckten Wörter in die Lücken ein.

1 speak for a **minority** / ____________

2 an unfair **advantage** / ____________

3 admire the **sunset** / ____________

4 House prices have **fallen** / ____________ .

5 live in a **wealthy** / ____________ city

6 **legal** / ____________ immigrants

7 have **more** / ____________ money for clothes

8 think of a **synonym** / an ____________

9 be **alive** / ________________

10 a **hopeful** / __________ situation

11 announce a **death** / __________

12 Was it built in 70 **AD** /or 70 __________ ?

13 He **appeared** / ____________ suddenly.

14 **forget** / ____________ a person's name

13 More about ... Los Angeles

Vervollständige den Text mit den Wörtern aus der Box.

The city of *El Pueblo de Nuestra Señora la Reina de Los Angeles del Rio de Porciuncula* was __________ (1) in 1781 by 44 Spanish-speaking settlers. Today we __________ (2) the city by the much shorter name of Los Angeles or L.A. The population of the city itself is now __________ (3) 4 million, while another 13 million people __________ (4) in the Los Angeles *metropolitan area. L.A. is California's largest city and the second __________ (5) in the US. The metropolitan area is over 12,000 square kilometres, almost half the __________ (6) of Belgium. People from all over the world live in L.A. The two __________ (7) languages are English and Spanish, but over 200 other languages are also spoken. L.A. is one of the world's most important economic centres. Everyone knows that it is a __________ (8) in the entertainment industry: thousands of films, TV shows and video games are all made there, and music __________ (9) plays a big role. But L.A. is also an important __________ (10) for business, trade and fashion.

metropolitan area = Ballungsraum

14 Lost words

Ergänze die Sätze mit den Wörtern rechts.

1 I don't really like his attitude __________ money.

2 Are people here prejudiced __________ immigrants?

3 In basketball, being tall gives you an advantage __________ other players.

4 After two hours, firefighters succeeded __________ putting the fire out.

5 How can we prevent people __________ littering the streets?

6 Computer prices have fallen __________ 10% in this year.

7 When are you going to introduce me __________ your parents?

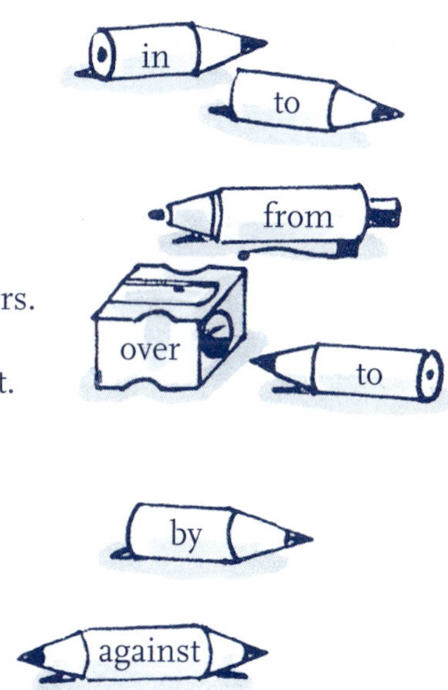

Unit 4

New words ▸pp. 76–78

You need a lot of grapes for ______________ .	Man braucht viele Trauben für die **Weinherstellung**.
Would you prefer to drink red or white ________ ?	Würdest du lieber Rot- oder Weiß**wein** trinken?
Kids start ______________ school at six.	Kinder fangen mit 6 Jahren in der **Grund**schule an.
____________ comes before elementary school.	Der **Kindergarten** kommt vor der Grundschule.
Doing sport is good for your ______________ .	Sport zu treiben, ist gut für die **Gesundheit**.
The prime minister leads the ______________ .	Der Premierminister führt die **Regierung**.
read announcements on the ______________	Bekanntgaben am **Schwarzen Brett** lesen
Pack warm ______________ and winter boots.	Pack warme **Kleidung** und Winterstiefel ein.
These shoes hurt – they're much too ________ !	Diese Schuhe tun weh – sie sind viel zu **eng**!
I looked through a ________________ wall.	Ich guckte durch eine **durchsichtige** Wand.
Be careful or you'll ________ your shirt.	Sei vorsichtig, oder du **zerreißt** dir das Hemd.
You mustn't ____________ the school rules.	Du darfst nicht gegen die Schulregeln **verstoßen**.
We all have to ________ the law.	Wir müssen alle dem Gesetz **gehorchen**.
This is only a __________ of Leonardo's painting.	Dies ist nur eine **Kopie** von Leonardos Gemälde.
Sorry, but the top isn't ____________ in size 4.	Leider ist das Oberteil nicht in Größe 4 **vorrätig**.

1 Hidden words

Ergänze die Wortgruppen, indem du Wörter mit Buchstaben des Wortes „kindergarten" bildest.

2 Pronunciation

Ordne die Wörter aus der Box der richtigen Aussprachegruppe zu.

aɪ	ɪ	iː

assignment biological casino clothing environment
giant insect kindergarten machine pizza police
rise routine sick still tight technique vineyard

rise	still	police

3 Last letter – first letter

Der letzte Buchstabe von jedem Wort ist gleichzeitig der erste des nächsten Wortes.

1 Handschuhe
2 Sweatshirt
3 Oberteil
4 Schlafanzug
5 Hemd
6 Hose
7 Anzug
8 Turnschuhe
9 kurze Hose
10 Rock
11 Strumpfhose
12 Socken

New words ▸ p. 79

This __________ leads to your classroom.	Dieser **Gang** führt zu deinem Klassenzimmer.
What time is the __________ with the boss?	Wann findet die **Besprechung** mit dem Chef statt?
It's boring here because there's so ______ to do.	Es ist langweilig hier, weil es so **wenig** zu tun gibt.
Do you really ________ me to believe you?	**Erwartest** du wirklich, dass ich dir glaube?
I'm going to ____ a doctor like my mum.	Ich **werde** Ärztin, wie meine Mutter auch.
He has ten years' teaching __________ .	Er hat zehn Jahre Unterrichts**erfahrung**.
Relax! The doctor is very __________ .	Entspann dich! Der Arzt ist sehr **erfahren**.
Which job do you want to __________ for?	Für welchen Job willst du dich **bewerben**?
Too few people __________ in politics.	Zu wenig Menschen **engagieren sich** in der Politik.
Dan is ________ tall ___ Jake: both are 181 cms.	Dan ist **genauso** groß **wie** Jake: beide sind 181 cms.

4 Spot the mistakes

In jedem Satz sind zwei Fehler. Unterstreiche und korrigiere sie.

1 After greeting the gests I introjuced them to each other. guests __________
2 Use a hankerchief to wipe the sweat off your forhead. __________ __________
3 Think about your helth and try and loose some weight. __________ __________
4 Please don't ly on the grass – it's still wett after the rain. __________ __________
5 If you brake the rules, you'll be in troble. __________ __________
6 The local vineyards are trying a new methode of making vine. __________ __________

5 The fourth word

Welches Wort fehlt hier?

1 boy – boys	man – men	6 students – student	children – __________
2 hand – hands	foot – __________	7 hamsters – hamster	mice – __________
3 robber – robbers	thief – __________	8 husbands – husband	wives – __________
4 fox – foxes	wolf – __________	9 eyes – eye	teeth – __________
5 star – stars	hero – __________	10 tests – test	quizzes – __________

New words ▸ pp. 80–81

J. F. Kennedy's ______________ were Irish.	J. F. Kennedys **Vorfahren** waren Iren.
Some immigrants return to their __________ .	Manche Einwanderer gehen zurück ins **Heimatland**.
Lübeck is a UNESCO world-__________ city.	Lübeck ist UNESCO Welt**erbe**stadt.
The park opens daily ____________ the year.	Der Park hat **das ganze** Jahr **hindurch** geöffnet.
He sticks all his postcards in a ____________ .	Er klebt all seine Postkarten in ein **Sammelalbum**.
Bad Arolsen is Hermann's ______________ .	Bad Arolsen ist Hermanns **Partnerstadt**.
_______ the invitation ___ to everyone else, please.	Bitte **leite** die Einladung an alle anderen **weiter**.
Who'll help with the __________ to my new flat?	Wer hilft beim **Umzug** in meine neue Wohnung?
He's too old for the job. It can't ____________ .	Er ist zu alt für die Stelle. Das kann nicht **gutgehen**.
You have to be __________ to survive the winter.	Man muss **hart** sein, um den Winter zu überleben.
You have to ______________ to new situations.	Man muss **sich** an neue Situationen **gewöhnen**.

6 Word friends

In jedem Haus gibt es drei Wörter bzw. Wortverbindungen, die man direkt nach dem Verb auf der Fahne benutzen kann. Unterstreiche sie.

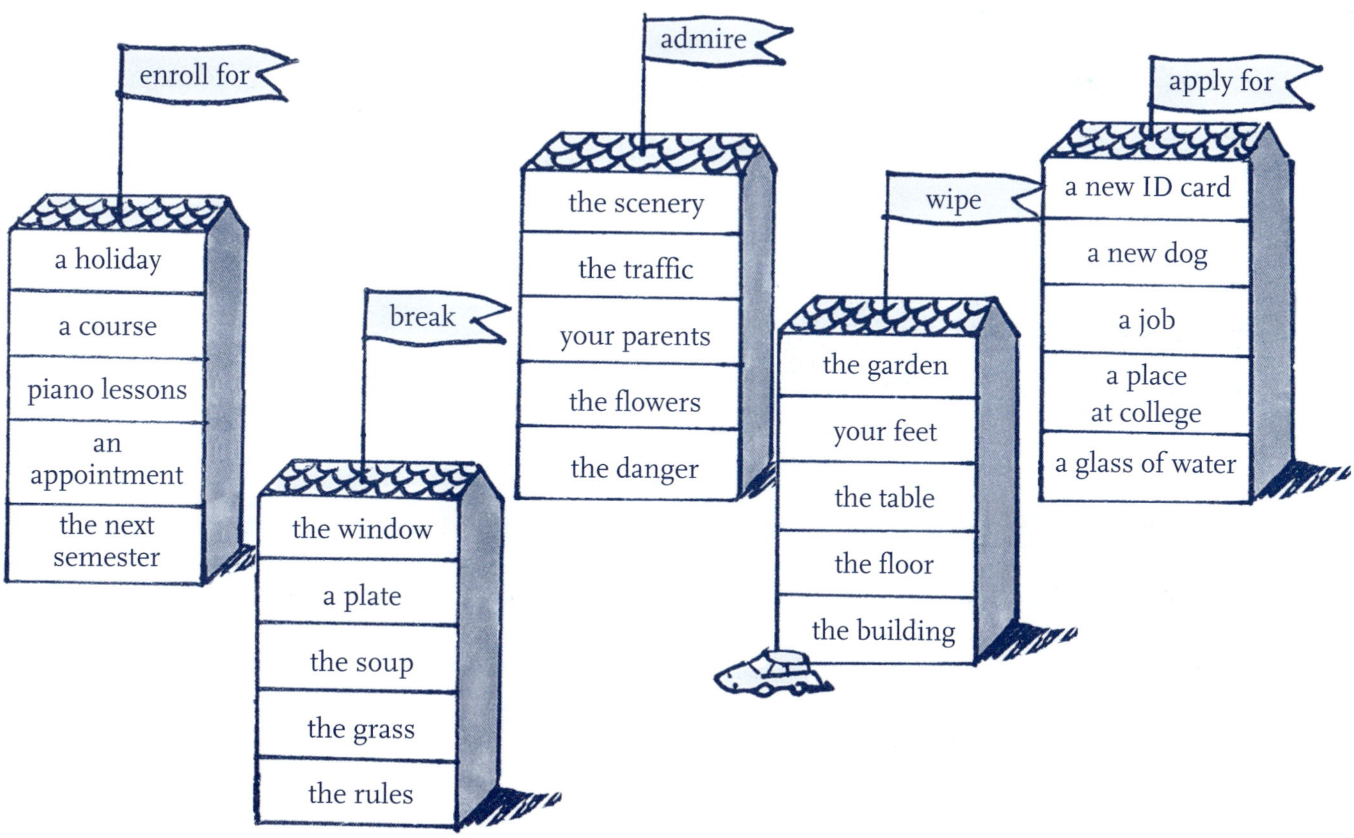

New words ▸ pp. 85–89

At the end of a letter you write ______________ .	Am Briefende steht *Mit freundlichen Grüßen.*
Sausages taste much better with ______________ .	Würstchen schmecken viel besser mit **Senf**.
Dad likes lots of ______________ on his bread.	Papa mag viel **Butter** auf seinem Brot.
Please ______________ that the light is out.	**Vergewissere dich** bitte, dass das Licht aus ist.
He often ______________ terrible headaches.	Er **leidet** oft **an** schrecklichem Kopfweh.
I only read a ______________ of the report.	Ich las nur eine **Zusammenfassung** des Berichts.
This is a copy. The ______________ is in London.	Dies ist eine Kopie. Das **Original** ist in London.
I prefer the new version to the ______________ one.	Ich ziehe die neue Version der **ursprünglichen** vor.

7 Crossword

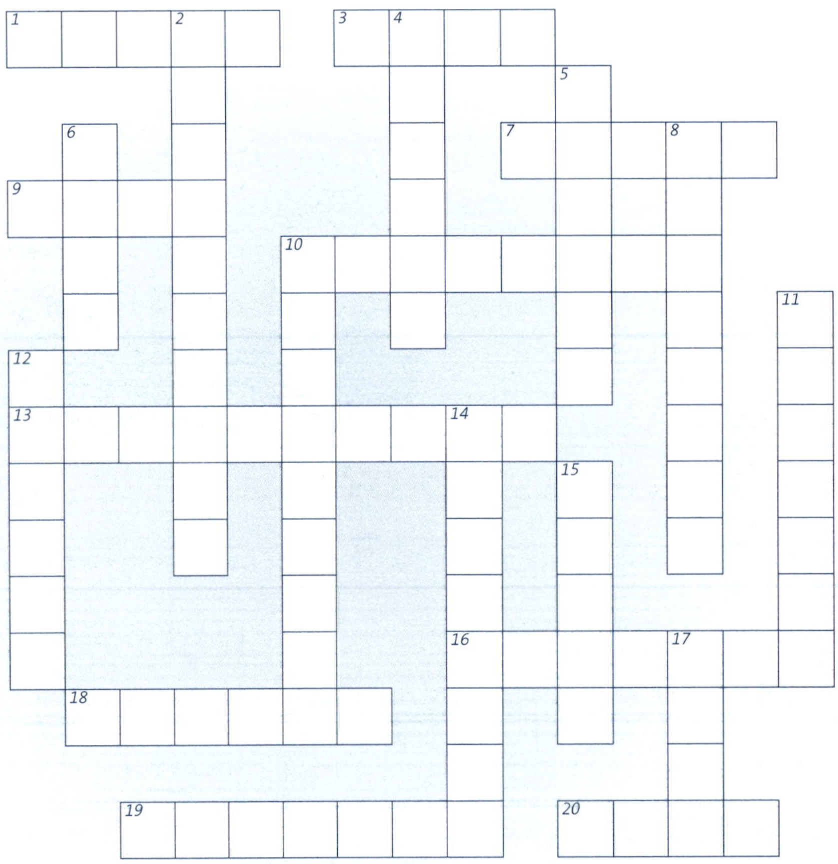

Across

1 schwierig, hart (5)
3 (zer)reißen (4)
7 eng, fest (5)
9 Umzug (4)
10 Vorfahr/in (8)
13 Erlebnis, Erfahrung (10)
16 Korridor, Gang (7)
18 leiden (6)
19 Besprechung, Versammlung (7)
20 gehorchen (4)

Down

2 Regierung (10)
4 erwarten, annehmen (6)
5 wenig (6)
6 Kopie, Abschrift (4)
8 Erbe (8)
10 erhältlich (9)
11 Zusammenfassung (7)
12 Gesundheit (6)
14 Kleidung (8)
15 sich bewerben, beantragen (5)
17 Wein (4)

New words ▸ *p. 90*

You'll get ________ if you eat chips all the time.	Du wirst **dick**, wenn du immer Pommes isst.
That's really ________________ . It can't be true!	Das ist echt **unglaublich**! Es kann nicht wahr sein.
Goalkeepers need very good ______________ .	Torhüter brauchen sehr gute **Reflexe**.
People say that foxes are ______________ animals.	Man sagt, dass Füchse **schlaue** Tiere sind.
We ______________ a new parliament every 5 years.	Wir **wählen** alle 5 Jahre ein neues Parlament.
Which party won the ________________ ?	Welche Partei hat die **Wahl** gewonnen?
I'm tired, but ________________ I want to stay up.	Ich bin müde, aber **irgendwie** will ich aufbleiben.
Would you ___________ for or against this law?	Würdest du für oder gegen dieses Gesetz **stimmen**?
They ____________________ and married soon after.	Sie **verliebten sich** und heirateten bald danach.
If you have toothache, go to the ______________ .	Wenn du Zahnschmerzen hast, geh zum **Zahnarzt**.
We play basketball in the school ___________ .	Wir spielen Basketball in der Schul**turnhalle**.

8 More about ... German immigrants in North America

Vervollständige den Text mit den Wörtern aus der Box.

among
ancestors
as
escape
first
improve
Jewish
millions
newspapers
number
religious
sailed

Since the 17th century, ______________ (1) of Germans have left Europe to make new homes in North America. In 1683 in Pennsylvania, 13 families founded the _____________ (2) German town in the New World: they called it Germantown. By 1750, there were about 45,000 Germans in Pennsylvania alone. During the next century, the ______________ (3) of immigrants continued to grow. They left Germany partly to find ______________ (4) or political liberty, but mainly to ______________ (5) their economic situation. Over a million people ______________ (6) to the US after the *failed revolution of 1848. In the 19th century, New York City was popular ______________ (7) German immigrants. By 1860 over 100,000 Germans lived there. There were 50 German schools, 20 churches, at least 10 bookshops and two German language daily ______________ (8). In the 1930s there were many ______________ (9) immigrants, among them Albert Einstein, who had to leave Germany to ______________ (10) from the Nazis. After World War II, Germans continued to go the US, but the numbers weren't ___________ (11) high as before. Today about 58 million Americans say that they have German ___________ (12).

failed = gescheitert

New words ▸ *pp. 91–92*

After three glasses of wine she felt _______ .	Nach drei Gläsern Wein fühlte sie sich **betrunken**.
Tell me the worst! _________________ !	Sag mir das Schlimmste! **Ich kann's aushalten**!
You often go red if you're _____________ .	Man wird oft rot, wenn man **verlegen** ist.
It's _______________ to cry in public.	Es ist **peinlich**, in der Öffentlichkeit zu weinen.
Do people go to ___________ when they die?	Kommt man in den **Himmel**, wenn man stirbt?
I felt sick, and I had to _______________ .	Mir war schlecht, und ich musste mich **übergeben**.
If you _____ me a _________ , I'll help you too.	Wenn du mir einen **Gefallen tust**, helfe ich dir auch.
All the band's fans _________ and cheered .	Alle Fans der Band **klatschten** und jubelten.
The 1906 __________ destroyed San Francisco.	Das **Erdbeben** von 1906 zerstörte San Francisco.
Big crowds ___________ against the new law.	Große Mengen **protestierten** gegen das neue Gesetz.
Who's your _____________ in the next match?	Wer ist dein **Gegner** im nächsten Spiel?
Boxers fight with their ___________ .	Boxer kämpfen mit ihren **Fäusten**.

9 Word search

Finde in dem Gitter 18 Begriffe zum Thema „Familie". Schreibe dann das Wort und die deutsche Übersetzung auf. (↓ →)

Q	D	Y	C	C	J	P	E	T	L	X	C	P
G	M	O	T	H	E	R	C	W	M	E	M	A
G	I	H	I	U	I	S	S	I	S	T	E	R
X	C	O	U	S	I	N	N	N	K	H	W	E
B	S	Y	J	B	E	G	P	S	I	S	O	N
V	X	G	F	A	G	G	F	P	R	P	S	T
F	G	R	A	N	D	P	A	R	E	N	T	S
B	N	A	C	D	H	O	T	Q	L	D	M	D
A	U	N	T	J	X	X	H	F	A	K	B	R
U	M	D	N	A	N	C	E	S	T	O	R	L
U	L	C	N	X	A	L	R	D	I	I	O	N
N	B	H	B	B	S	S	Y	R	V	M	T	W
C	H	I	L	D	F	W	I	F	E	P	H	M
L	C	L	V	W	B	W	R	K	P	M	E	M
E	L	D	A	U	G	H	T	E	R	T	R	B

mother – Mutter

10 Definitions

Vervollständige die Definitionen mit Wörtern aus der linken Sprühwolke. Trage die Lösungen aus der anderen Sprühwolke in die rechte Spalte ein.

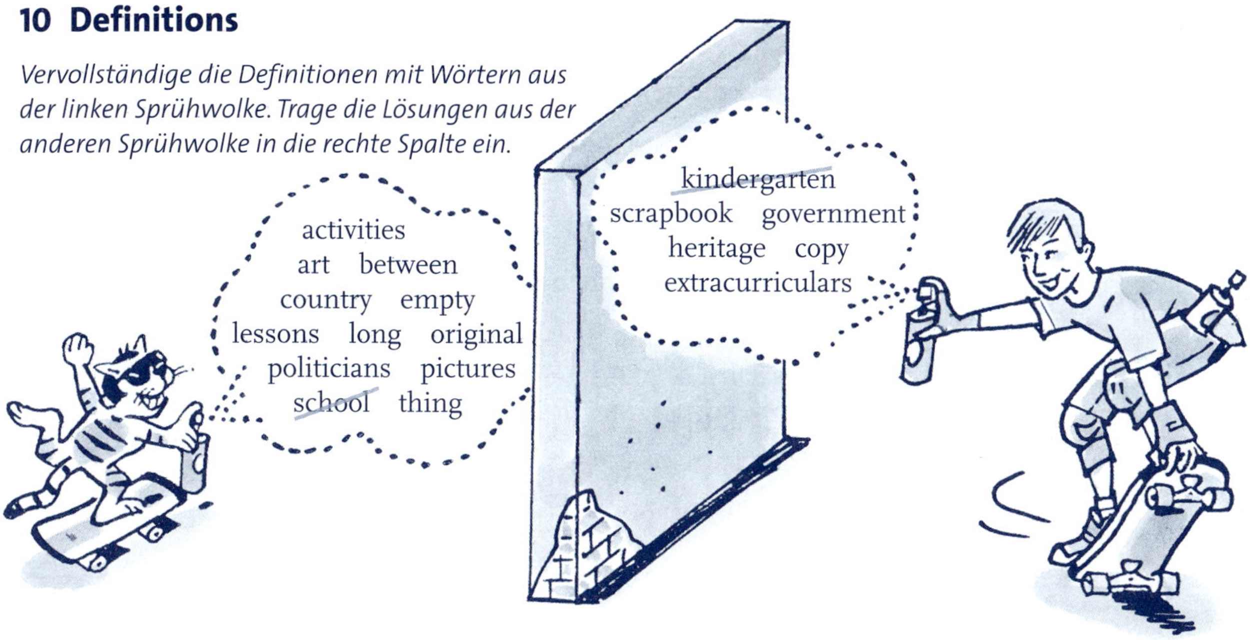

1 a kind of school for children ______ 4 and 6 years. kindergarten

2 a group of ______ who lead a ______ ______

3 a ______ that is made so that it looks like the ______ ______

4 ______ you can do at school when ______ are over ______

5 a book with ______ pages where you can stick ______ ______

6 a country's traditions, ______, architecture, etc. over a ______ time ______

11 Scrambled words: American and British English

Die Buchstabenrätsel ergeben Wörter aus dem amerikanischen Englisch. Trage diese und ihre britischen Entsprechungen ein. Die Tipps helfen dir.

		American English	British English	tip
1	**norc**	corn		food for cattle or people
2	**doas**			Better to drink water than this!
3	**moortres**			Sometimes you have to go here.
4	**pipincarl**			top man or woman at a school
5	**issmagnnet**			work after school
6	**tiress ticy**			town with link to another town
7	**liblunet droab**			Information hangs here.
8	**screes**			time to relax between lessons

Unit 5

New words ▸pp. 98–99

The American __________ began in 1861.	Der amerikanische **Bürgerkrieg** begann 1861.
__________ are wide roads between cities.	**Autobahnen** sind breite Straßen zwischen Städten.
build streets as a __________ system	Straßen wie ein **Gitter**netz bauen
The logo of the __________ is 5 rings.	Das Logo der **Olympischen Spiele** sind 5 Ringe.
be a member of the __________ movement	ein Mitglied der **Bürgerrechts**bewegung sein
We have the __________ to speak freely.	Wir haben das **Recht** frei zu sprechen.
The __________ leads the city government.	Der **Bürgermeister** führt die Stadtregierung.
CNN is a big American TV __________ .	CNN ist ein großer amerikanischer TV-**Sender**.

1 Word ladder

Gehe von unten nach oben, indem du auf jeder Sprosse einen Buchstaben veränderst.

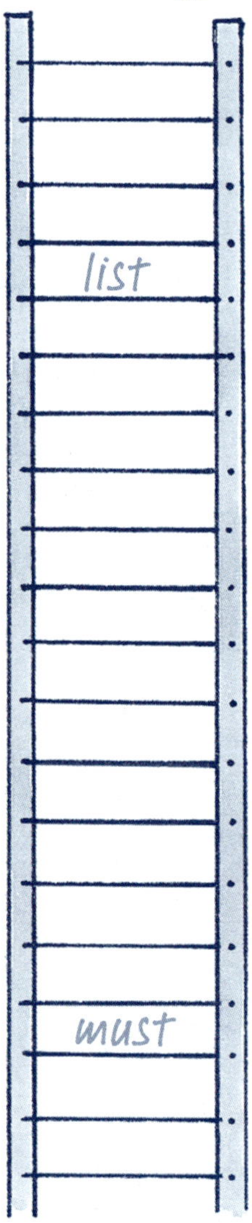

It's so beautiful here. I ★ we could stay for ever.
I'm sorry, but you aren't allowed to ★ in this lake.
He hit me in the face with his ★ !
Here's a ★ of the people I want to invite to my party.
Shall we use the stairs or the ★ ?
The murderer was given a ★ sentence.
That isn't Mr Smith's ★ . It's his sister.
Please put that bottle of ★ in the fridge.
Please ★ the table before you lay it.
You can't eat those apples yet. They aren't ★ !
With the help of a ★ , the prisoner was able to escape.
Sue's got a fantastic ★ in the school play.
You could lose something through that ★ in your pocket.
The firefighter picked up his ★ and started to put the fire out.
Atlanta was ★ to the Olympic Games in 1996.
That's the ★ incredible story I've ever heard.
You ★ show ID when you're getting onto the plane.
There's so much ★ in this room. Why hasn't it been cleaned?
Are you sure you're OK? – Yes, I'm fine ... ★ a bit tired.

New words ▸ *pp. 100–101*

____________ collect news.	**Nachrichtenagenturen** sammeln Nachrichten.
Dad's favourite TV ________ is the news.	Die Nachrichten sind Papas Lieblings-TV-**Sendung**.
I like ______ series and talk shows.	Ich mag **Fernsehspiele** und Talkshows.
The match will be _________ live on TV.	Das Spiel wird im Fernsehen live **übertragen**.
Can you ______ the radio to 102,3 FM?	Kannst du das Radio auf 102.3 FM **einstellen**?
Were you nervous? – ______ ! Very nervous!	Warst du nervös? – **Und ob!** Sehr nervös sogar!
It's so late. I ___________ gone earlier.	Es ist so spät! Ich **hätte** früher gehen **sollen**.
I don't like it and ______ it's too expensive.	Ich mag es nicht, und **außerdem** ist es zu teuer.
You look sad, Mum. _________ ?	Mama, du siehst traurig aus. **Was ist los?**
Was *The Lord of the Rings* ______ in Scotland?	Wurde *Der Herr der Ringe* in Schottland **gedreht**?
I'll drive you to the ferry and ____ you __ there.	Ich fahre dich zur Fähre und **setze** dich dort **ab**.
First, the teacher ________ us __ the topic.	Zuerst **führte** uns der Lehrer in das Thema **ein**.
He's too shy to ________ in discussions.	Er ist zu scheu, um an Diskussionen **teilzunehmen**.
The dog buried the ______ in the garden.	Der Hund hat den **Knochen** im Garten vergraben.

2 Word groups: Sports

Trage die Wörter aus der Box in die richtigen Listen ein.

~~champion~~ cheerleader climbing coach court footballer goalkeeper hiking hunting ice rink pitch pool referee riding running track sailing skating ski slope skiing stadium supporter

people

champion
______
______
______
______
______
______

places

______
______
______
______
______
______
______

activities

______
______
______
______
______
______
______

New words ▸ p. 102

The painting is ______________ in the museum.	Das Gemälde ist im Museum **ausgestellt.**
Today is the first ______________ of his death.	Heute ist der erste **Jahrestag** seines Todes.
I'm ______________ ! You can paint really well.	Ich bin **beeindruckt!** Du kannst echt gut malen.
I can do the photo research in the ______________ .	Ich kann die Fotorecherche im **Archiv** machen.
______________ in South Africa ended in 1994.	Die **Rassentrennung** in Südafrika endete 1994.
Blacks were often ______________ from whites.	Schwarze wurden oft von Weißen **getrennt**.
Everyone should be ______________ before the law.	Alle Menschen sollten vor dem Gesetz **gleich** sein.
I like ______________ films, without blood.	Ich mag **gewaltfreie** Filme, ohne Blut.
She was the victim of a ______________ attack.	Sie war das Opfer eines **gewalttätigen** Angriffs.
There's a lot of crime and ______________ on TV.	Im Fernsehen gibt es viel Verbrechen und **Gewalt**.
To ______________ goods is a kind of protest.	Waren zu **boykottieren** ist eine Art Protest.
The students are organizing a protest ______________ .	Die Studenten organisieren einen Protest**marsch**.
Don't ______________ somebody by the car he drives.	**Beurteile** niemanden nach dem Auto, das er fährt.
A hat helps to protect your ______________ from the sun.	Ein Hut hilft, die **Haut** vor der Sonne zu schützen.
He said he wasn't bored, ______________ tired.	Er sagte, er sei nicht gelangweilt, **sondern** müde.
A hero is usually a strong ______________ .	Ein Held ist meistens eine starke **Persönlichkeit**.

3 Spot the mistakes

In jedem Satz sind zwei Fehler. Unterstreiche und korrigiere sie.

1 Most zivil wars take place in poorer countrys. civil ______________

2 A major is a leader of a city goverment. ______________ ______________

3 The litters BBC stand for British Brodcasting Corporation. ______________ ______________

4 The aniversary of Beethoven's daeth is March 26. ______________ ______________

5 The internationale news network CNN was found in Atlanta. ______________ ______________

6 Maybe you'll find the informations you need in the city archiv. ______________ ______________

7 Jake is going to interduce me to his parants next week. ______________ ______________

8 What did you think of the main charakter in the drame? ______________ ______________

New words ▸ p. 103

Will he arrive in time? Is he ______________ ?	Wird er rechtzeitig kommen. Ist er **zuverlässig**?
I'm ___________ paper and plastics for recycling.	Ich **sortiere** Papier und Plastik für das Recyclen.
Her age is in ______________ after her name.	Ihr Alter steht in **Klammern** nach ihrem Namen.
Read the ______________ at the end of the page.	Lesen Sie die **Fußnoten** am Ende der Seite!
The car is in the underground ______________ .	Das Auto steht auf dem unterirdischen **Parkplatz**.
You're in a hurry. I don't want to __________ you.	Du hast es eilig. Ich will dich nicht **aufhalten**.
After a ten-minute __________ our plane started.	Das Flugzeug startete nach 10 Minuten **Verspätung**.
The house was destroyed by a gas ____________ .	Das Haus wurde durch eine **Gasexplosion** zerstört.
The rescue team were ______________ quickly.	Der Rettungsdienst war schnell **zur Stelle**.

4 Word search

Finde im Rätsel 18 Begriffe zum Thema Politik und Gesellschaft. Schreibe jedes Wort und die deutsche Übersetzung auf. (↓ →)

P	R	I	M	E	M	I	N	I	S	T	E	R	P	S
R	O	Y	I	N	J	T	N	P	E	K	U	E	B	V
E	N	L	N	F	P	O	I	O	G	I	P	V	F	G
S	B	G	O	V	E	R	N	O	R	X	W	O	K	O
I	G	P	R	V	R	Q	J	K	E	P	R	L	X	V
D	A	R	I	G	H	T	I	V	G	K	B	U	S	E
E	W	C	T	S	M	S	Y	I	A	S	K	T	E	R
N	E	H	Y	A	P	O	L	I	T	I	C	I	A	N
T	M	N	B	P	A	X	N	W	I	S	S	O	E	M
R	L	I	B	E	R	T	Y	L	O	X	T	N	H	E
O	F	L	D	G	L	V	H	X	N	E	B	K	R	N
M	A	J	O	R	I	T	Y	H	G	C	O	H	L	T
A	E	D	P	E	A	J	Y	R	M	A	Y	O	R	X
R	V	E	Y	E	M	X	B	B	U	E	C	B	E	E
C	R	A	A	D	E	L	E	C	T	I	O	N	F	O
H	V	F	G	G	N	Q	Q	K	R	M	T	H	I	P
W	O	M	V	O	T	E	N	P	R	O	T	E	S	T

president – Präsident

New words ▸ pp. 106–110

Your ______ time is 17.45, from Gate 7.	Ihre **Abflug**zeit ist 17.45, vom Flugsteig 7.
Grandpa has an ______ pocket watch.	Opa hat eine **altmodische** Taschenuhr.
Dad loves ______ like *Robinson Crusoe.*	Papa mag **Prosaliteratur** wie *Robinson Crusoe.*
I read ______ , on wildlife for example.	Ich lese **Sachliteratur**, z.B. über die Tierwelt.
What are the ______ of modern art?	Welche **Merkmale** hat die moderne Kunst?
I didn't know that. Nobody ______ me.	Ich wusste das nicht. Keiner hat mich **informiert.**
This book ______ social problems.	Dieses Buch **handelt von** sozialen Problemen.
They want to sing to ______ their guests.	Sie wollen singen, um ihre Gäste zu **unterhalten**.
A. C. Doyle wrote famous detective ______ .	A. C. Doyle schrieb berühmte Detektiv**romane.**
Many people say politics don't ______ them.	Viele sagen, dass Politik sie nicht **interessiert.**
He was buried after the ______ .	Nach der **Trauerfeier** wurde er beerdigt.
It was a non-violent march, not a ______ .	Es war ein gewaltfreier Marsch, keine **Krawalle.**
Each ethnic group has its own ______ .	Jede ethnische Gruppe hat eine eigene **Identität.**

5 Hour glasses

Übersetze die Wörter und trage sie in die passende Sanduhr ein.

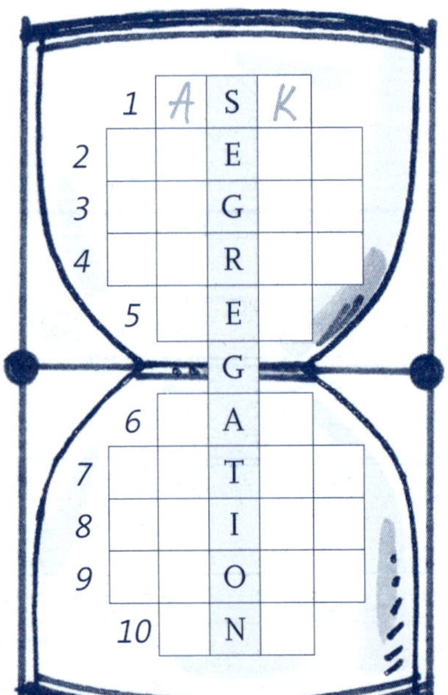

1 Spion – bitten
2 wählen – Fernsehspiel
3 Recht – Demonstration
4 betreten – Strophe
5 nähen – binden
6 Lippe – Gesetz
7 Spiel – beantragen
8 schlau – Lack
9 (Film) drehen – später
10 (irgend)welche – gelangen

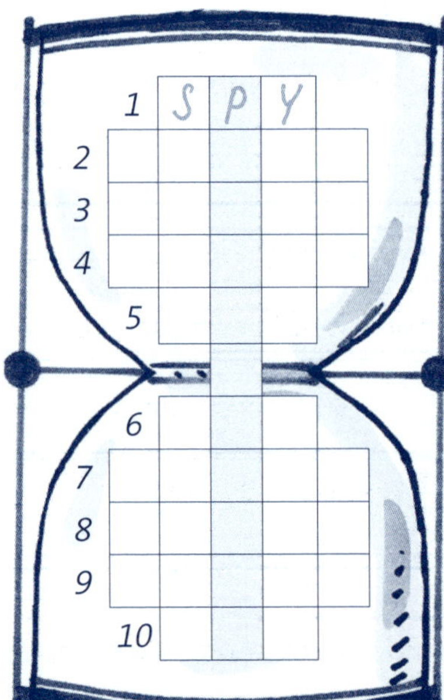

Das geheime Wort in der rechten Sanduhr heißt: *Englisch* ______

Deutsch ______

6 More about … The Atlanta Olympics

Vervollständige den Text mit den Wörtern aus der Box.

anniversary
be
case
crowd
for
from
just
money
over
special
than
were

'And the winner is … .' Six cities had wanted to hold the 1996 Olympics: Athens, Atlanta, Belgrade, Manchester, Melbourne and Toronto. Many people expected that Melbourne or Toronto would __________ (1) chosen. But after the final round of voting, the winner was Atlanta – a __________ (2) victory, because 1996 was the 100th ______________ (3) of the modern Olympic Games.

Getting ready __________ (4) the Olympic Games always takes a long time – in Atlanta's __________ (5) it took six years – and the preparations cost billions of dollars. The city didn't __________ (6) have to build a new stadium and other sports *venues. It also spent a lot of __________ (7) on improving the city centre with new streets and parks. On July 19th 1996, the Games __________ (8) opened by President Clinton in front of a __________ (9) of 83,000 people. During the next seventeen days, over 10,000 athletes __________ (10) 197 nations participated in the Games. More __________ (11) 2 million visitors came to Atlanta and about 3.5 billion people all ________ (12) the world followed the event on TV. *venue= Austragungsort*

7 Lost words

Ergänze die Sätze mit den Wörtern rechts.

1 Please inform us __________ any changes to your plans.
2 This novel deals __________ the everyday life of ethnic minorities.
3 You should never judge a book __________ its cover.
4 Jake wants to introduce me __________ his parents.
5 There's a march to protest ____________ the plans for a motorway.
6 You can pass the book __________ to Jack after you've finished it.
7 How many runners participated ________ last year's Marathon?
8 Which party are you going to vote ____________ in the election, Dad?
9 Mum sometimes suffers ____________ bad headaches.
10 I suppose she'll fall in love ____________ the hero and marry him.

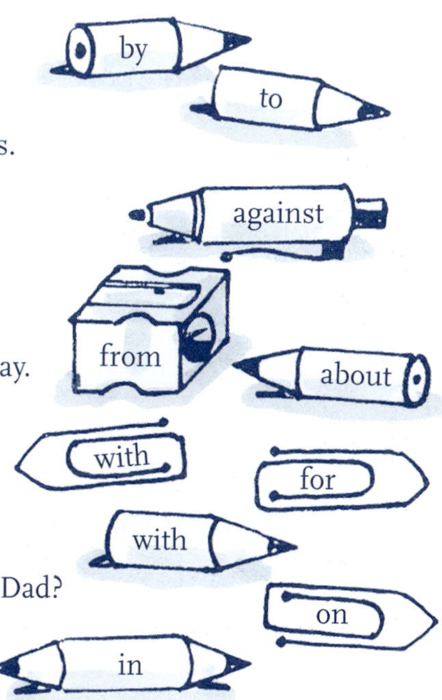

New words ▸ pp. 111–112

Liberty or ________________ ! That is our choice!	Freiheit oder **Sklaverei**! Das ist unsere Wahl!
It fell __________ like a house of cards.	Es fiel wie ein Kartenhaus **auseinander**.
The café has a ____________ room for smokers.	Das Café hat einen **getrennten** Raum für Raucher.
If you print that, I'll take you to ____________ .	Wenn Sie das drucken, bringe ich Sie vor **Gericht**.
When he moved away, I lost __________ with him.	Als er wegzog, verlor ich den **Kontakt** zu ihm.
Only small kids ride the ____________________ .	Nur kleine Kinder fahren auf dem **Karussell**.
Good morning _____ ! Can I help you?	Guten Morgen, **Sir**! Kann ich Ihnen helfen?
He acted __________ nothing had happened.	Er tat, **als ob** nichts geschehen wäre.
Help! I'm ______________________ spiders.	Hilfe! Ich **habe schreckliche Angst vor** Spinnen.
If he gets worse, call a doctor _______________ .	Wenn es ihm schlechter geht, ruf **sofort** den Arzt.
Did nobody _________________ to help you?	Hat **sich** keiner **bereit erklärt**, dir zu helfen?
There are 22 ____________ to the next floor.	22 **Stufen** führen zum nächsten Stock.
Ice and snow _______________ many roads.	Eis und Schnee **blockierten** viele Straßen.
They __________ murderers in some countries.	In manchen Ländern werden Mörder **gehängt**.

8 Words with the same meaning

Finde in der Box Wörter, die dieselbe Bedeutung haben wie die fettgedruckten Wörter. Trage sie ein und schreibe die deutsche Übersetzung auf.

dependable gym immediately nearly ~~reply~~ sick smart tough wealthy

1	I promised to **answer**/ reply **straightaway** / ________________ .	sofort
2	They're quite **rich** / ____________ , but they never show their money.	____________
3	We need somebody really **reliable** / ____________________ for this job.	____________
4	Jo's **clever** / ____________ enough not to make the same mistake twice.	____________
5	If you feel **ill** / ____________ , maybe you should stay at home today.	____________
6	Hurry up! It's **almost** / ____________ time to leave.	____________
7	Sue's gone to **sports hall** / ____________ to do some stomach exercises.	____________
8	It was a **difficult** / ____________ test, but I got quite a good mark.	____________

New words ▸ *pp. 113–114*

He's ____________ with his bad grades.	Er ist von seinen schlechten Noten **enttäuscht**.
We'll ____________ our fans if we lose.	Wir **enttäuschen** unsere Fans, wenn wir verlieren.
He ____________ lots of gold across the border.	Er hat viel Gold über die Grenze **geschmuggelt**.
His eyes were hard and ____________ .	Seine Augen waren hart und **grausam**.
A horse ____________ him and broke his leg.	Ein Pferd **trat** ihn und brach ihm das Bein.
The egg tasted bad and he ____________ it out.	Das Ei schmeckte schlecht und er **spuckte** es raus.
He grabbed my ________ and pulled me away.	Er packte mein **Handgelenk** und zog mich weg.
Bad weather ____________ us to give up.	Schlechtes Wetter **zwang** uns aufzugeben.
Water ____________ against the windscreen.	Wasser **spritzte** gegen die Windschutzscheibe.
Lemons contain more ____________ than apples.	Zitronen enthalten mehr **Säure** als Äpfel.
Students ____________ after 11 years.	Schüler **machen den Schulabschluss** nach 11 Jahren.
I ____________ to hear that you're well.	Ich **freue mich** zu hören, dass es dir gut geht.
We'll have to try and ____________ the problem.	Wir müssen versuchen, das Problem zu **lösen**.
Have we got the ________ to pay for the project.	Haben wir die **Mittel**, um das Projekt zu bezahlen.
Many people lost money in the bank ________ .	Viele Leute verloren Geld in der Banken**krise**.
What was his ____________ to the news?	Wie war seine **Reaktion** auf die Nachrichten?

9 The best word

Finde in jeder Schublade das Wort, das am besten in die Lücke passt.

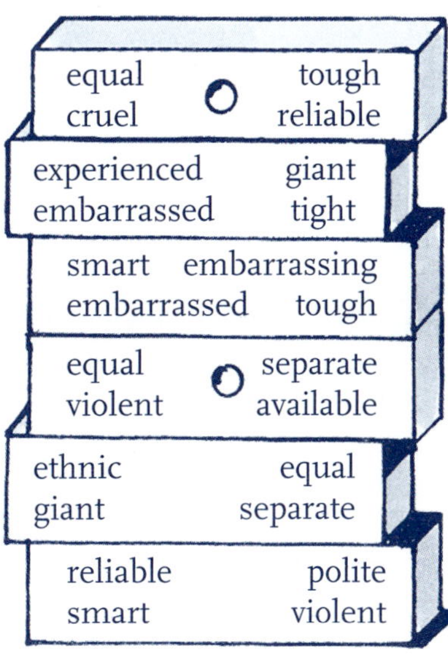

1 I don't understand why some people are ____________ to animals.

2 If you apply for this job, you should be ____________ .

3 You needn't feel ____________ if you don't know the answer.

4 Sorry, but the book you're looking for isn't ____________ any more.

5 All people should have a(n) ____________ chance in life.

6 If he has promised to help, he will – he's very ____________ .

10 Crossword

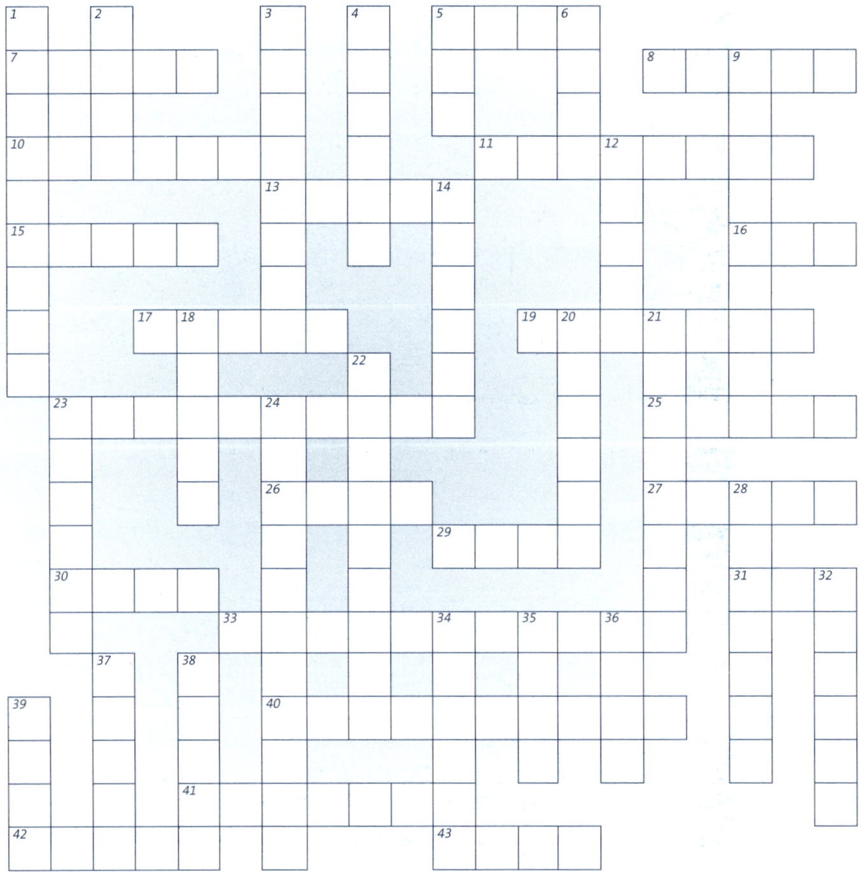

Across

5 shake – shook / bleed – ★ (4)
7 the leader of an Indian tribe (5)
8 not moving and quiet (5)
10 very good, great (7)
11 colonists who came to America in 1620 (8)
13 a bird needs them to fly (5)
15 the time a baby is born (5)
16 place to do sport (3)
17 There's no ★ without a fire. (5)
19 BE – motorway / AE – ★ (7)
23 person who writes about news for the media (10)
25 go in (5)
26 part of the body between head and shoulders (4)
27 The Sioux are a Native American ★. (5)
29 change the place where you live (4)
30 forgive – forgiven / lie – ★ (4)
31 part of the mouth (3)
33 verb – celebrate / noun – ★ (11)
40 very tall building (10)
41 Speaking to a big crowd would make me ★. (7)
42 person who flies a plane (5)
43 meet – meeting / sell – ★ (4)

Down

1 book in which you can stick pictures (9)
2 money you must pay if you break the law (4)
3 AE – assignment / BE – ★ (8)
4 India was a British ★ until 1947. (6)
5 You need it to shoot arrows. (3)
6 Often young girls play with it. (4)
9 person who has come to live in a country (9)
12 deep valley (5)
14 the time when the sun goes down (6)
18 a walk to protest against something (5)
20 read something again to prepare for a test (6)
21 meet – meeting / elect – ★ (8)
22 You can use this word at the end of a letter. (9)
23 area of tropical forest (6)
24 date that people remember because of what happened on the same date in the past (11)
28 opposite of legal (7)
32 sing – song / pray – ★ (6)
34 BE – break / AE – ★ (6)
35 broken – break / torn – ★ (4)
36 do what you are told to do (4)
37 a long written story (5)
38 another word for huge (5)
39 opposite of high (4)

Introduction

1 Word families

a) *1* friendly, *2* colourful, *3* different, *4* horrible, *5* cloudy, *6* electric, *7* dangerous, *8* daily, *9* public, *10* crowded

b) *1* friendly, *2* difference, *3* colourful, *4* public, *5* horror

2 Word search

O	C	V	A	L	L	E	Y	G	W	J	I
B	O	I	C	S	F	O	R	E	S	T	S
E	C	L	W	A	T	E	R	F	A	L	L
A	A	L	A	K	E	C	L	I	F	F	A
C	N	A	S	C	E	N	E	R	Y	H	N
H	A	G	X	I	D	X	T	S	I	I	D
R	L	E	E	I	W	R	O	C	K	L	T
I	G	U	C	T	O	P	A	R	K	L	U
V	O	J	O	M	O	U	N	T	A	I	N
E	R	W	A	J	D	X	O	K	M	T	N
R	G	W	S	K	S	E	A	A	Q	X	E
L	E	Q	T	T	Z	D	V	P	K	I	L

valley – Tal, **forest** – Wald, **waterfall** – Wasserfall, **lake** – See, **cliff** – Klippe, **scenery** – Landschaft, **rock** – Felsen, **park** – Park, **mountain** – Berg, **sea** – Meer, **beach** – Strand, **river** – Fluss, **canal** – Kanal, **gorge** – Schlucht, **village** – Dorf, **coast** – Küste, **woods** – Wald, **hill** – Hügel, **island** – Insel, **tunnel** – Tunnel

3 Spot the mistakes

1 for: four, visits: visit
2 traps: trips, accomodation: accommodation
3 heiks: hikes, diffrent: different
4 from: of, threw: through
5 reservat: reservation, awsome: awesome

4 The best word

1 glad, *2* colourful, *3* public, *4* deep, *5* ultimate, *6* daily

5 More about ... The Grand Canyon Skywalk

1 kind, *2* shape, *3* sticks, *4* allowed, *5* through, *6* take, *7* special, *8* tribe, *9* public, *10* includes, *11* popular, *12* build

6 Last letter – first letter

1 accommodation, *2* neat, *3* tribe, *4* editor, *5* reservation, *6* neighbour, *7* rim, *8* match, *9* hike, *10* exciting, *11* glad

7 Words in pictures: outdoor activities

1 boots – hiking
2 saddle – riding
3 paddle – canoeing / paddling
4 swimming trunks / swimsuit – swimming
5 bike – cycling
6 tent – camping
7 skis – skiing
8 running shoes – running
9 skateboard – skating
10 racket – tennis

8 Odd word out

1 border, *2* toes, *3* accommodation, *4* glad, *5* tribe, *6* mule, *7* include, *8* awful, *9* dinosaur, *10* especially

9 Scrambled words: American and British English

1 kilometer, kilometre
2 gas, petrol
3 grade, class
4 awesome, great
5 auto, car

10 Crossword

1 G	L	A	D						2 H	
O					3 P		4 R	U	I	N
5 R	O	6 C	K		U				K	
G		A			7 B	O	R	D	E	8 R
E		T			L					I
	9 S	T	R	A	I	G	H	10 T		M
		L			C			R		
	11 T	E	N	12 T		13 D	A	I	L	Y
	O			I		E		B		
	O			14 P	R	E	F	E	R	
	L					P				

Unit 1

1 Number crossword – Revision

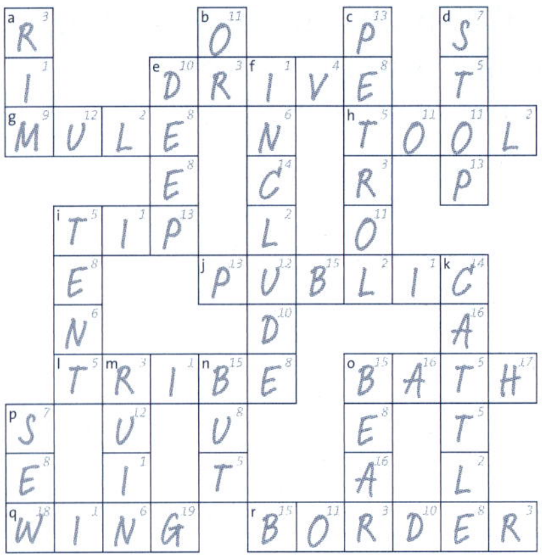

öffentlich – **j** across
Vieh – **k** down
Maultier – **g** across
Grenze – **r** across
Zelt – **i** down
Benzin – **c** down
Rand, Kante – **a** down
Flügel – **q** across
Werkzeug – **h** across
wetten – **n** down
einschließen – **f** down
anhalten – **d** down
Badewanne – **o** across
Spitze – **i** across

2 Hidden words

1 pair, *2* deep, *3* trip,
4 tired, *5* part, *6* pirate,
7 rat, *8* air, *9* star, *10* pie, *11* eastern

3 Definitions

1 live – country: immigrate
2 safer – busy: pedestrian crossing
3 line – cars: queue
4 guests – party: hostess
5 pay – wrong: fine
6 streets – public: litter
7 planes – fly: wings
8 deep – rocks: gorge

4 Opposites

1 ... far–distance–Entfernung
2 ... sad–feeling–Gefühl
3 ... quiet–sound–Klang
4 ... early–time–Zeit
5 ... cool–temperature–Temperatur
6 ... small–size–Größe
7 ... white–colour–Farbe
8 ... old–age–Alter

5 Word search - In a city

S	S	D	O	W	N	T	O	W	N	H	W
T	I	S	K	Y	S	C	R	A	P	E	R
A	D	H	M	Z	M	U	S	E	U	M	C
T	E	O	B	Y	S	Y	Q	Z	M	J	R
U	W	S	K	G	R	Y	U	Y	M	Q	O
E	A	P	F	A	Y	C	A	R	L	B	S
R	L	I	O	U	K	Z	R	Q	I	R	S
D	K	T	S	N	U	C	E	M	B	I	W
W	F	A	P	V	F	J	M	V	R	D	A
C	O	L	A	V	E	N	U	E	A	G	L
H	U	A	R	B	L	O	C	K	R	E	K
B	A	N	K	S	U	B	W	A	Y	H	E

downtown – Stadtzentrum,
skyscraper – Hochhaus,
museum – Museum,
avenue – Allee, **block** – (Wohn-)Block,
bank – Bank, **subway** – U-Bahn,
statue – Statue, **sidewalk** – Gehweg, **hospital** – Krankenhaus, **park** – Park, **square** – Platz,
library – Bücherei, **bridge** – Brücke,
crosswalk – Fußgängerüberweg

6 Pronunciation

ɔː – also, call, sidewalk, war
ɑː – grass, path, raft, start
ə – breakfast, binoculars, distance, ultimate
æ – avenue, cattle, gas, map
eɪ – grade, immigrate, sale, take

7 The fourth word

1 lobby, *2* wings, *3* foot, *4* dollar, *5* mile,
6 tall, *7* first floor, *8* below, *9* middle school,
10 burn, *11* petrol station, *12* immigrant,
13 fish, *14* dish, *15* police station, *16* sale

8 Lost words

1 wherever, *2* myself, *3* itself, *4* whatever,
5 yourself, *6* whoever, *7* wherever,
8 herself, *9* whenever, *10* themselves

9 Word ladder

hike – **like** – line – fine – find – kind –
king – wing – wind – mind –mine –
mile – mule – male – sale

10 Word building

1 **cream cheese** – Frischkäse
2 **teaspoon** – Teelöffel
3 **ticket office** – Kasse
4 **training session** – Trainingsstunde, -einheit
5 **number plate** – Nummernschild
6 **petrol station** – Tankstelle
7 **sunglasses** – Sonnenbrille

8 **street performer** – Straßenkünstler(in)
9 **fireman** – Feuerwehrmann
10 **fire station** – Feuerwache

11 Scrambled words: American and British English

1 grade, class, *2* subway, underground, *3* sidewalk, pavement, *4* line, queue, *5* downtown, city centre, *6* apartment, flat, *7* crosswalk, pedestrian crossing, *8* neighbor, neighbour

12 Words with different meanings

1 **flat** – Wohnung/flach,
2 **fine** – Geldstrafe/gut,
3 **service** – Service/Gottesdienst,
4 **stop** – Aufenthalt/aufhören,
5 **tip** – Spitze/Tipp,
6 **tall** – hoch/groß
7 **floor** – Boden/Stockwerk,
8 **break** – Pause/Kaputt machen

13 More about ... Remembering 9/11

1 skyline, *2* you, *3* touch, *4* close, *5* work, *6* on, *7* whole, *8* help, *9* who, *10* although

14 Hour glasses

1		A	S	K	
2	T	O	P	I	C
3	C	R	E	A	M
4	L	O	C	A	L
5		A	T	E	
			A		
6		I	C	E	
7	D	O	U	G	H
8	P	I	L	O	T
9	D	R	A	F	T
10		C	R	Y	

1		F	O	G	
2	C	A	B	I	N
3	T	A	S	T	E
4	S	W	E	A	T
5		T	R	Y	
			V		
6		M	A	D	
7	E	N	T	E	R
8	B	L	O	C	K
9	M	A	R	R	Y
10		B	Y	E	

Das geheime Wort lautet:
Englisch – observatory
Deutsch – Aussichtsplattform

15 Verb forms

2 sew – sewed – sewn
3 leave – left – left
4 ring – rang – rung
5 come – came – come
6 forgive – forgave – forgiven
7 blow – blew – blown
8 cut – cut – cut
9 feel – felt – felt
10 wake – woke – woken

16 Word friends

fill: your glass, a room , a cake
taste: delicious, the soup, awful
enter: the room, the United States, a building
take over: a plane, a bank, a company
revise: an essay, grammar, for a test

17 What are the words?

1 sich verändern, *2* umtauschen, *3* umschalten, *4* sich umziehen, *5* umsteigen, *6* wechseln

18 Word groups

food and drink
bagel, beef, coffee, cream cheese, dough, onion, roll, salmon
lines of work
firefighter, hairdresser, hostess, journalist, musician, pilot, politician
religion
blessing, cathedral, church, mass, mosque, saint, service, synagogue
roads and paths
avenue, cycle path, highway, pavement, pedestrian crossing, street, trail

Unit 2

1 Last letter – first letter

1 doll, *2* ladder, *3* religious, *4* smoke, *5* extraordinary, *6* yawn, *7* noble, *8* exciting, *9* goat, *10* turkey, *11* young, *12* gloves, *13* spring, *14* goal, *15* lip

2 Word search

H	O	U	R	M	I	B	A	C	O	N	U	S	W	E	X	M
W	N	O	Y	T	C	J	C	H	I	L	D	P	P	D	X	A
W	I	N	D	O	W	Q	A	I	I	I	B	W	O	M	A	N
N	O	I	S	M	P	S	K	C	A	R	R	O	T	X	D	C
D	N	U	Y	A	J	A	Y	K	D	L	O	J	A	T	O	R
B	U	L	E	T	T	U	C	E	U	F	O	E	T	R	O	F
U	D	W	R	O	S	S	T	N	L	C	F	L	O	O	R	X
P	A	S	T	E	A	A	S	L	T	G	J	N	V	I	R	B
K	Y	V	U	X	A	G	D	S	T	E	A	K	B	A	L	A
H	G	P	R	E	S	E	N	T	G	N	F	B	V	W	G	P
R	L	B	K	W	Q	Q	V	A	B	F	Q	B	E	A	N	U
Y	R	P	E	N	U	G	M	I	N	U	T	E	F	L	Y	B
F	O	F	Y	E	A	R	L	R	D	T	T	E	H	L	T	A
U	O	S	B	S	S	H	T	S	V	U	W	F	L	N	J	B
Y	M	O	N	T	H	A	Q	B	T	R	L	A	O	U	G	Y
Y	O	R	T	H	H	A	A	T	E	E	N	A	G	E	R	U

house
door, window, floor, room, stairs, roof, wall
time
day, hour, past, present, minute, year, month, future
humans
man, child, woman, teenager, adult, baby
meat
turkey, bacon, steak, sausage, chicken, beef
vegetables
bean, carrot, lettuce, onion, tomato, squash, potato

3 Hidden words
1 cola, *2* oil, *3* lane, *4* learn, *5* boat, *6* article, *7* clean, *8* bacon, *9* table, *10* actor

4 More about … Traditional Native American homes
1 kinds, *2* called, *3* skill, *4* took, *5* by, *6* could, *7* enough, *8* possible, *9* themselves, *10* open

5 Lost words
1 with, *2* on, *3* to, *4* on, *5* on, *6* with, *7* in, *8* of, *9* to, *10* of

6 Word families
a) *1* shoot, *2* celebrate, *3* cause, *4* speak, *5* revise, *6* fill, *7* taste, *8* die, *9* immigrate, *10* collect, *11* sell, *12* compare
b) *1* cause, *2* revise, *3* death, *4* celebrate, *5* speech

7 Crossword

1 B		2 P		3 T	U	R	K	4 E	Y			5 B	
R		A						N		6 S	O	I	L
7 A	R	R	O	W				T				R	
V		A			8 C	E	L	E	B	R	A	T	E
E		D						R				H	
		9 E	X	H	I	B	I	T	I	O	N		
10 S								A					
M			11 I				12 P	I	L	G	R	I	M
13 O	P	I	N	I	O	N		N					
K			T					M			14 S		
15 E	F	F	E	C	T			E			P		16 B
			R			17 G		N			R		I
	18 A	G	R	I	C	U	L	T	U	R	E		B
19 H			U			I					A		L
U			P			D		20 C	A	N	D	L	E
21 G	O	A	T			E							

8 Hour glasses

1		T	I	P	
2	G	A	M	E	S
3	H	U	M	A	N
4	C	H	I	E	F
5		A	G	E	
			R		
6		G	A	S	
7	A	F	T	E	R
8	S	A	I	N	T
9	S	H	O	O	T
10		A	N	D	

1		A	C	T	
2	S	M	O	K	E
3	F	E	N	C	E
4	W	A	S	T	E
5		G	E	T	
			Q		
6		N	U	T	
7	Q	U	E	U	E
8	F	I	N	A	L
9	N	I	C	E	R
10		K	E	Y	

Das geheime Wort lautet:
Englisch – consequence
Deutsch – Folge, Konsequenz

9 Spot the mistakes
1 tableclothe: tablecloth, ley: lay
2 Maiz: Maize, food: feed
3 effekts: effects, smokeing: smoking
4 interupt: interrupt, wile: while
5 vers: verse, peom: poem
6 staf: staff, spezific: specific

10 The best word
1 secret, *2* spectacular, *3* perfect, *4* hopeless, *5* extraordinary, *6* mean

11 Odd word out
1 arrow, *2* maize, *3* turkey, *4* hedgehog, *5* staff, *6* harvest, *7* sale, *8* fault, *9* brave, *10* rude, *11* settler, *12* colony

12 Definitions
1 arms – hold: hug, *2* play – baby: doll
3 up – ground: spring, *4* fun – event: celebrate
5 new – region: settlers, *6* work – school: staff

13 Words with the same meaning
1 journey/trip – Reise
2 flat/apartment – Wohnung
3 close to/near – nahe (bei)
4 subject/topic – Thema
5 fans/supporters – Fans
6 sort/kind – Art
7 afraid/scared – Angst haben
8 hard/difficult – schwierig

14 Word ladder
fill – **will** – wild – mild – milk – mile – mole – hole – hold – gold – good – food – foot – **boot** – boat – goat

15 Word pairs
found – college, grow – corn, shoot – bear, milk – cow, lift – chair, cause – problems, commit – crime, spread – news, share – money, sentence – murderer, interrupt conversation, celebrate – birthday, shake – hands

16 Pronunciation
ə: revolution, colony, commit, opinion, period, victory

ɒ: politics, colonist, consequence, doll, shot, tablecloth

əʊ: grow, hopeless, rope, smoke, soldier, protest

17 Word friends
keep
quiet, your eyes on the baby, smiling
shoot
a film, foxes, yourself in the foot
give
me a smile, a speech, me a hug
share
a secret, a room, your ideas
grow
up in a city, tomatoes, very slowly

Unit 3

1 Words with different meanings
1 right – richtig/rechts,
2 mean – bedeuten/gemein,
3 spring – Frühling/Quelle,
4 counter – Theke/Spielstein,
5 lift – hochheben/Fahrstuhl,
6 wave – Welle/winken,
7 put – formulieren/hinlegen
8 subject – Schulfach/Staatsangehöriger

2 The fourth word
1 president, *2* disadvantage, *3* illegal, *4* minority, *5* homeless, *6* education

3 Word groups
farm animals
cattle, chicken, cow, goat, horse, sheep, turkey
education
college, grade, high school, semester, student, teacher, term, test
cinema
box office, crime film, director, documentary, happy ending, movie, scene
social relations
discrimination, ethnic group, immigrant, majority, minority, population, prejudice, segregation
IT (information technology)
computer, crash, download, e-mail, monitor, online forum, software, webcam, website
the coast
cliff, harbour, rock, sea, tide, waves

4 Word ladder
mark – dark – bark – **Park** – part – cart – care – case – **cake** – wake – wave – have

5 Number crossword
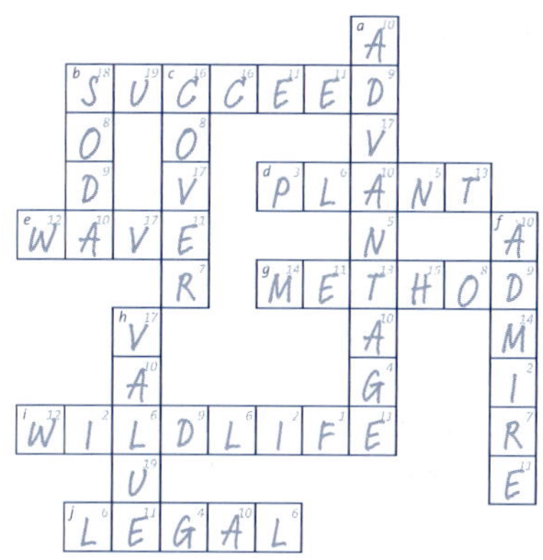

bewundern – **f** down
Vorteil – **a** down
Erfolg haben – **b** across
Wert – **h** down
Methode – **g** across
pflanzen – **d** across
zudecken – **c** down
legal – **j** across

6 Word search
I	A	T	R	A	I	N	S	B	S	P	N	U	G
N	T	T	R	Z	H	O	L	I	D	A	Y	S	E
F	T	U	M	H	O	T	R	K	K	C	Q	J	M
O	R	X	A	O	O	O	R	J	O	K	P	O	C
R	A	R	P	T	Z	U	L	Y	H	N	L	U	A
M	C	E	A	E	C	R	I	Y	D	U	A	R	R
A	T	S	T	L	S	I	G	H	T	S	N	N	A
T	I	T	T	M	U	S	E	U	M	T	E	E	V
I	O	A	Z	T	E	T	R	T	R	I	P	Y	A
O	N	U	B	I	H	T	P	T	E	N	T	O	N
N	H	R	C	C	P	A	S	S	E	N	G	E	R
O	X	A	A	K	L	S	O	U	V	E	N	I	R
L	C	N	M	E	W	G	C	W	I	U	A	Q	Q
G	T	T	P	T	N	Y	N	N	Q	O	Z	J	T

train – Zug, **holidays** – Ferien, **sights** – Sehenswürdigkeiten, **museum** – Museum, **trip** – Ausflug, **tent** – Zelt, **passenger** – Passagier,

souvenir – Mitbringsel,
information – Information,
attraction – Sehenswürdigkeit,
restaurant – Restaurant, **map** – Stadtplan,
camp – Ferienlager, **hotel** – Hotel,
ticket – (Fahr-)Karte, **tourist** – Tourist,
pack – packen, **plane** – Flugzeug,
journey – Reise, **caravan** – Wohnwagen

7 Odd word out

1 coach, *2* wildlife, *3* monitor, *4* caption,
5 shake, *6* soda, *7* plain, *8* advantage,
9 get along, *10* tease

8 Word families

1 warning, *2* confusion,
3 thought, *4* plant,
5 success, *6* discrimination,
7 blood, *8* waste,
9 ownership, *10* prayer,
11 sentence, *12* hug

9 The best word

1 perfect, *2* hopeless, *3* secret,
4 illegal, *5* noble, *6* specific

10 Hour glasses

1		I	C	E	
2	A	M	O	N	G
3	V	A	L	U	E
4	H	I	L	L	Y
5		F	O	X	
			C		
6		L	A	W	
7	F	E	T	C	H
8	G	U	I	D	E
9	D	R	O	W	N
10		E	N	D	

1		S	E	W	
2	O	W	N	E	R
3	C	O	V	E	R
4	D	R	I	V	E
5		T	R	Y	
			O		
6		E	N	D	
7	L	I	M	I	T
8	O	C	E	A	N
9	S	I	N	C	E
10		A	T	E	

Das geheime Wort lautet:
Englisch – environment, Deutsch – Umwelt

11 Verb forms

2 sweep – swept – swept
3 rise – rose – risen
4 bleed – bled – bled
5 grow – grew – grown
6 lead – led – led
7 cost – cost – cost
8 feel – felt – felt
9 spread – spread – spread
10 shake – shook – shaken
11 throw – threw – thrown
12 speak – spoke – spoken
13 fall – fell – fallen
14 teach – taught – taught
15 put – put – put
16 make – made – made

12 Opposites

1 majority, *2* disadvantage, *3* sunrise,
4 risen, *5* poor, *6* illegal, *7* less,
8 antonym, *9* dead, *10* hopeless,
11 birth, *12* BC, *13* disappeared,
14 remember

13 More about ... Los Angeles

1 founded, *2* know,
3 about, *4* live,
5 largest, *6* size,
7 main, *8* leader,
9 also, *10* centre

14 Lost words

1 to, *2* against, *3* over,
4 in, *5* from, *6* by, *7* to

Unit 4

1 Hidden words

1 read, *2* great, *3* tree, *4* king, *5* earring,
6 green, *7* greet, *8* tiger, *9* Greek,
10 knee

2 Pronunciation

aɪ – rise, assignment, biological, environment, giant, tight
ɪ – still, clothing, insect, kindergarten, sick, vineyard
iː – police, casino, machine, pizza, routine, technique

3 Last letter – first letter

1 gloves, *2* sweatshirt, *3* top, *4* pyjamas,
5 shirt, *6* trousers, *7* suit, *8* trainers,
9 shorts, *10* skirt, *11* tights, *12* socks

4 Spot the mistakes

1 gests: guests, introjuced: introduced
2 hankerchief: handkerchief, forhead: forehead
3 helth: health, loose: lose
4 ly: lie, wett: wet
5 brake: break, troble: trouble
6 methode: method, vine: wine

5 The fourth word

1 men, *2* feet, *3* thieves, *4* wolves, *5* heroes,
6 child, *7* mouse, *8* wife, *9* tooth, *10* quiz

6 Word friends

1 enroll for: a course, piano lessons, the next semester
2 break: the window, a plate, the rules
3 admire: the scenery, your parents, the flowers
4 wipe: your feet, the table, the floor
5 apply for: a new ID card, a job, a place at college

7 Crossword

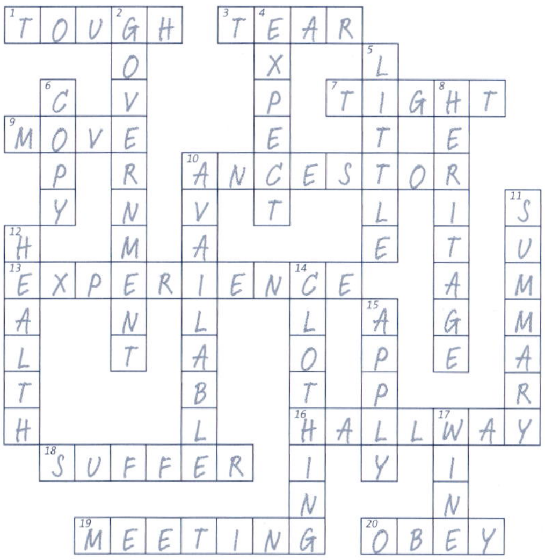

8 More about... German immigrants in North America

1 millions, *2* first, *3* number, *4* religious, *5* improve, *6* sailed, *7* among, *8* newspapers, *9* Jewish, *10* escape, *11* as, *12* ancestors

9 Word search

Q	D	Y	C	C	J	P	E	T	L	X	C	P
G	M	O	T	H	E	R	C	W	M	E	M	A
G	I	H	I	U	I	S	S	I	S	T	E	R
X	C	O	U	S	I	N	N	N	K	H	W	E
B	S	Y	J	B	E	G	P	S	I	S	O	N
V	X	G	F	A	G	G	F	P	R	P	S	T
F	G	R	A	N	D	P	A	R	E	N	T	S
B	N	A	C	D	H	O	T	Q	L	D	M	D
A	U	N	T	J	X	X	H	F	A	K	B	R
U	M	D	N	A	N	C	E	S	T	O	R	L
U	L	C	N	X	A	L	R	D	I	I	O	N
N	B	H	B	B	S	S	Y	R	V	M	T	W
C	H	I	L	D	F	W	I	F	E	P	H	M
L	C	L	V	W	B	W	R	K	P	M	E	M
E	L	D	A	U	G	H	T	E	R	T	R	B

mother – Mutter, **sister** – Schwester, **cousin** – Cousin, Cousine, **son** – Sohn, **grandparents** – Großeltern, **aunt** – Tante, **ancestor** – Vorfahre, **child** – Kind, **wife** – Ehefrau, **daughter** – Tochter, **uncle** – Onkel, **grandchild** – Enkel/in, **husband** – Ehemann, **father** – Vater, **twins** – Zwillinge, **relative** – Verwandte(r), **brother** – Bruder, **parents** – Eltern

10 Definitions

1 school – between: kindergarten
2 politicians – country: government
3 thing – original: copy
4 activities – lessons: extracurriculars
5 empty – pictures: scrapbook
6 art – long: heritage

11 Scrambled words: American and British English

1 corn, maize
2 soda, lemonade
3 restroom, toilet
4 principal, head teacher
5 assignment, homework
6 sister city, twin town
7 bulletin board, notice board
8 recess, break

Unit 5

1 Word ladder

just – dust – **must** – most – host – hose – hole – role – rope – ripe – wipe – wine – wife – life – lift – **list** – fist – fish – wish

2 Word groups

people
champion, cheerleader, coach, footballer, goalkeeper, referee, supporter
places
court, ice rink, pitch, pool, running track, ski slope, stadium
activities
climbing, hiking, hunting, riding, sailing, skating, skiing

3 Spot the mistakes

1 zivil: civil, countrys: countries,
2 major: mayor, goverment: government,
3 litters: letters, Brodcasting: Broadcasting,
4 aniversary: anniversary, daeth: death,
5 internationale: international, found: founded,
6 informations: information, archiv: archive
7 interduce: introduce, parants: parents,
8 charakter: character, drame: drama

4 Word search

P	R	I	M	E	M	I	N	I	S	T	E	R	P	S
R	O	Y	I	N	J	T	N	P	E	K	U	E	B	V
E	N	L	N	F	P	O	I	O	G	I	P	V	F	G
S	B	G	O	V	E	R	N	O	R	X	W	O	K	O
I	G	P	R	V	R	Q	J	K	E	P	R	L	X	V
D	A	R	I	G	H	T	I	V	G	K	B	U	S	E
E	W	C	T	S	M	S	Y	I	A	S	K	T	E	R
N	E	H	Y	A	P	O	L	I	T	I	C	I	A	N
T	M	N	B	P	A	X	N	W	I	S	S	O	E	M
R	L	I	B	E	R	T	Y	L	O	X	T	N	H	E
O	F	L	D	G	L	V	H	X	N	E	B	K	R	N
M	A	J	O	R	I	T	Y	H	G	C	O	H	L	T
A	E	D	P	E	A	J	Y	R	M	A	Y	O	R	X
R	V	E	Y	E	M	X	B	B	U	E	C	B	E	E
C	R	A	A	D	E	L	E	C	T	I	O	N	F	O
H	V	F	G	G	N	Q	Q	K	R	M	T	H	I	P
W	O	M	V	O	T	E	N	P	R	O	T	E	S	T

prime minister – Präsident/in
governor – Gouverneur/in
right – Recht
politician – Politiker/in
liberty – Freiheit
majority – Mehrheit
mayor – Bürgermeister/in
election – Wahl
vote – Stimme, Stimmrecht
protest – Protest
president – Präsident/in
march – Marsch, Demonstration
minority – Minderheit
parliament – Parlament
segregation – Trennung
boycott – Boykott
revolution – Revolution
government – Regierung

5 Hour glasses

1		A	S	K	
2	E	L	E	C	T
3	R	I	G	H	T
4	V	E	R	S	E
5		S	E	W	
			G		
6		L	A	W	
7	M	A	T	C	H
8	P	A	I	N	T
9	S	H	O	O	T
10		A	N	Y	

1		S	P	Y	
2	D	R	A	M	A
3	M	A	R	C	H
4	E	N	T	E	R
5		T	I	E	
			C		
6		L	I	P	
7	A	P	P	L	Y
8	S	M	A	R	T
9	L	A	T	E	R
10		G	E	T	

Das geheime Wort lautet:
Englisch – participate
Deutsch – teilnehmen

6 More about ... The Atlanta Olympics

1 be, *2* special, *3* anniversary, *4* for, *5* case, *6* just, *7* money, *8* were, *9* crowd, *10* from, *11* than, *12* over

7 Lost words

1 about, *2* with, *3* by, *4* to, *5* against, *6* on, *7* in, *8* for, *9* from, *10* with

8 Words with the same meaning

1 answer/reply – antworten, straightaway/immediately – sofort
2 rich/wealthy – reich
3 reliable/dependable – zuverlässig
4 clever/smart – schlau
5 ill/sick – krank
6 almost/nearly – fast
7 sports hall/gym – Sporthalle
8 difficult/tough – schwierig

9 The best word

1 cruel, *2* experienced, *3* embarrassed, *4* available, *5* equal, *6* reliable

10 Crossword